# GREAT CITIES

# VENICE

First American Edition published in 2004
by Enchanted Lion Books
115 West 18th Street, New York, NY 10011

ISBN 1–59270–014–4


LIBRARY OF CONGRESS CATALOGING-IN-PUBLICATION DATA
A CIP record for this book is available from the Library of Congress.

McRae Books Srl
Borgo S. Croce, 8, 50122 — Florence, Italy
info@mcraebooks.com

Text: Renzo Rossi
Illustrations: Andrea Ricciardi di Gaudesi, Manuela Cappon, Lorenzo
Cecchi, Lucia Mattioli, Luisa della Porta, Studio Stalio (Alessandro
Cantucci, Fabiano Fabbrucci, Andrea Morandi, Ivan Stalio)
Graphic Design: Marco Nardi
Layout: Yotto Furuya
Editors: Claire Moore, Anne McRae
Picture Research: Claire Moore
Cutouts: Filippo Delle Monache, Giampietro Bruno, Alman Graphic Design
Color Separations: Litocolor, Florence (Italy)

ACKNOWLEDGEMENTS
All efforts have been made to obtain and provide compensation for the
copyright to the photos and artworks in this book in accordance with
legal provisions. Persons who may nevertheless still have claims are
requested to contact the copyright owners.

t=top; tl=top left; tc=top center; tr=top right; c=center; cl=center left;
cr=center right; b= bottom; bl=bottom left; bc=bottom center; br=bottom right

The Publishers would also like to thank the following photographers and
picture libraries for the photos used in this book.

AFP Photo/Andrea Merola: 17br; AFP Photo/Vincenzo Pinto: 43br;
Archivi Alinari, Florence: 19tl, 29br, 34tl; Bianconero, Venice: 20cl, 35tl,
42bl; © Cameraphoto Arte - Venezia: 25tc, 29tc; Cinetext: 33bl, 43cr;
Corbis/Contrasto: 18b, 34–35b; Farabola Foto (The Bridgeman Art
Library): 9tl, 10bl, Bridgeman Art Library/Alinari 14tr, 19tr, 23cr, 26tl,
26b, Francesco Turio Bohm 27cl, 28b, 29tr, Lauros/Giraudon/Bridgeman
Art Library 32b, 34bc, Roger-Viollet, Paris 35cr, Giraudon/Bridgeman Art
Library 38tr, 38–39b; © Foto Scala, Firenze: 12–13b, 13r, 14b, 15b,
16cr, 22–23b, 23tr, 30bl, 40b; Lonely Planet Images: Juliet
Coombe/LPI 21c, 24c, Graham Tween/LPI 29bl, John Brettell/LPI 39tc,
Damien Simonis/LPI 40tc, 41bc, 43cl, Bethune Carmichael 43t; Marco
Nardi/McRae Books Archives: 11tr, 19c, 19br, 21tr, 21br, 24br, 28cl,
29cr, 31tr, 31bl, 34cl, 36bl, 37br, 39c, 40tl, 41tr, 42tl, 43bl, 43bc;
The Art Archive/Bodleian Library Oxford/The Bodleian Library - Bodley
264 folio 218r: 9b; The Image Works: 24tc, 37tc, 39tl; United
Artists/The Kobal Collection: 34tr.

Printed and bound in Belgium
1 2 3 4 5 / 09 08 07 06 05 04 03

# GREAT CITIES THROUGH THE AGES

# VENICE

## Renzo Rossi

Enchanted Lion Books
*New York*

Venice has some of the most beautiful buildings in the world, including the 15th-century Palazzo Contarini del Bovolo.

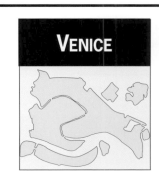

VENICE

**4th–6th centuries** Settlers begin to make their homes on the islands of the lagoon.

**697** The first doge takes office.

**828** The remains of St. Mark are brought to Venice.

# Table of Contents

The magnificent Doge's Palace (right) in St. Mark's Square was built between the 14th and 16th centuries.

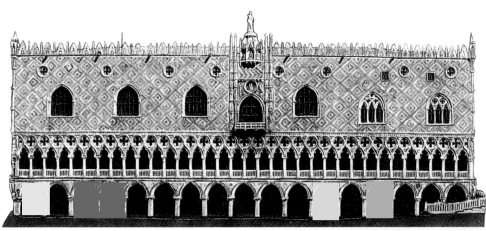

**Around 1000** Venice establishes itself as the main naval power in the Adriatic Sea.

**1094** St. Mark's Basilica is completed.

**1095** Venice becomes an important port for forces departing on the First Crusade.

**1104** The Arsenal is founded.

**1204** The Venetian navy raids Constantinople.

**1348** The Black Death strikes Venice.

**1516** Venice's Jewish inhabitants are confined to the Ghetto.

**1570s** Tintoretto and Veronese decorate the Doge's Palace.

**1588–91** The present Rialto Bridge is built across the Grand Canal.

**1638** Venice's first coffee house, the Caffé Quadri, opens.

**18th century** Artists such as Canaletto and composers like Vivaldi make Venice a fashionable place for visitors.

**1792** La Fenice opera house opens.

**1797** The last doge, Lodovico Manin, abdicates. The traditional Carnival

celebrations are outlawed.

**1846** A railroad bridge is built, joining Venice to the mainland.

**1895** The first Venice Biennale art exhibition is held.

**1932** The first Venice Film Festival is held.

**1960** Venice Airport opens.

**1966** Flooding of the city.

**1997** Rebuilding starts of La Fenice, after a fire in 1996.

**2003** Foundation stone laid for MOSE flood barrier.

Many statues adorn the campi (squares) of Venice, including this one of Bartolomeo Colleoni (1400–76).

# Introduction

The extraordinary beauty of Venice and the lagoon are as clearly visible to the modern visitor as they would have been to someone arriving in the city 500 years ago. From the medieval period through the 17th century, the Republic of Venice was one of the most prosperous communities in Europe, thanks to its important trade connections and sea power. That prosperity is still clearly reflected in the city's spectacular architecture, especially the Basilica and Doge's Palace in St. Mark's Square, and the sumptuous palaces along the Grand Canal. In the 15th and 16th centuries, Venetian painting, too, reached extraordinary heights in the vibrant colors and richly detailed works of Giovanni Bellini, Titian, and Tintoretto. By the 18th century, Venice's power was beginning to wane as trade patterns changed with the development of new sea routes and new markets. However, the city emerged as a fashionable, sophisticated playground for those rich enough to enjoy the many coffee houses, gambling clubs, and theaters, and it ranked high on the list of places to see for those making the "Grand Tour" of great European cities. Wealthy visitors were enraptured by the music of Vivaldi and many were not able to leave without taking a view of the city, maybe even one painted by Canaletto, as a souvenir. In the 19th century, many foreign artists and writers visited Venice, including poets such as Byron and Shelley and painters like Turner, Monet, and Renoir. By the 20th century, the city was firmly established as a resort, but events such as the Biennale art exhibition and the Venice Film Festival ensured that it remained a prestigious cultural center. Today, however, the conservation of Venice's magnificent heritage, and the fight against the *acqua alta* and pollution in the lagoon are an ever increasing challenge.

This glass goblet was made at the end of the 15th century by the celebrated glassmakers of Murano.

Doge Leonardo Loredan was one of over a hundred doges who ruled the city of Venice from the early 8th century until the fall of the Republic in 1797.

Built in 1846, the Ponte della Libertà stretches over 11,500 feet (3,500 m) and links Venice with mainland Italy.

**1ST CENTURY BC – 1100 AD**

**1st century BC** Venetia (the present Veneto, Friuli, and Trentino areas of Italy) is an administrative region of the Roman Empire.

**306–37** Constantine the Great reigns.

**337** First record of settlement in the Venetian lagoon.

**421** Venice is founded on April 25, St. Mark's Day.

**568** Lombard tribes begin invading Italy.

**639** The Cathedral of Torcello is founded.

**726** The first documented doge, Orso Ipato, is elected.

**810** Doge Angelo Partecipazio moves the seat of government from Malamocco to Rialto.

**814** Construction work starts on the Doge's Palace. Venice gains political and judicial independence from the Byzantine Empire.

**828** The remains of St. Mark are taken to Venice.

**832** St. Mark's Basilica is consecrated.

**840–41** The doge begins negotiating international trading agreements.

**1008** The Cathedral of Torcello is restored.

**1063–94** St. Mark's Basilica is rebuilt.

**1081** The Venetian navy goes to the aid of the besieged Byzantine emperor, Alexius Comnenus.

**1096–99** The First Crusade.

### Escaping the Lombards

The Lombards, a Germanic tribe, moved gradually south in the 5th century and by the end of the century were based in the area of modern-day Austria. In the spring of 568, they crossed the Alps and entered Italy. Their invasion of northern Italy was virtually unopposed and by 569 they had conquered most of the principal cities in the north. The Lombards drove great numbers of people living on mainland Italy to the islands of the Venetian lagoon, in search of refuge and safety. Gradually the population grew and economic activity began to develop in these isolated fishing areas, and by the 8th century, the islands were home to thriving communities.

Above: A detail of a Roman mosaic. Many huntsmen were also attracted to the lagoon, where they hunted game and wildfowl.

Left: This detail from a Lombard shield shows a horseman and his mount.

This mosaic shows the priest Theodore and the monk Stauracius giving St. Mark's body to the two Venetian merchants, Rustico di Torcello and Buono di Malamocco.

# Origins of the City

The earliest permanent settlements of the Venetian area date back to the decline of the Western Roman Empire in the 5th and 6th centuries, as the inhabitants of the Veneto took refuge on the islands in the lagoon from the invasions of the Lombards. Originally the home of fishermen and salt workers, the islands were suddenly faced with a surge in population and small villages were formed. In the 6th and 7th centuries, the Venetian lagoon was ruled by Byzantium, and building and trading activity flourished. By the time the body of St. Mark, Venice's patron saint, arrived in Venice in the early 800s, the political center had moved to the Rialto area. It was this move that saw the beginnings of the development of the Venice we know today, and the emergence of the city's classic shape and form.

### St. Mark Arrives in Venice

According to legend, the remains of the martyr, St. Mark the Evangelist, were transported from the Egyptian city of Alexandria to Venice by two Venetian merchants in 828. They hid his body under a layer of pork so Muslim officials would not investigate their goods too closely. The remains of St. Mark were initially kept in a chapel inside the Doge's Palace. Almost immediately he was proclaimed patron saint of the city, replacing the Greek St. Theodore.

### Lions of Venice

The Lion of Venice is the oldest symbol of the Venetian Republic and the official emblem of the city. Chosen as the city's defender in honor of St. Mark, Venetians customarily set up a stone lion in a strategic position in each of their territorial possessions.

The lion of St. Mark, the emblem of the city.

PAX TIBI MAR CE EVAN GELI STA MEVS

### Center of Power

The city's first administrative and political center was established on the island of Heraclea. It was later transferred to Malamocco and finally to the Rialto area. Lying above the water level of the lagoon, the Rialto quickly became a meeting place for merchants, tax collectors, and brokers. The real history of Venice, however, began with the election of the first doge, the chief magistrate of the city. Orso Ipato, the first documented doge, was elected in 726, but it is believed that Paolo Lucio Anafesto was installed even earlier, in 697.

The first Venetian coins were minted in 814. The one shown above dates to the 9th century.

This 16th-century drawing shows early settlements in the Rialto area.

## Control of the Adriatic

Venice's history of successful trading originated with the first waves of refugees from mainland Italy. Having constructed houses of wattle and daub on the lagoon islands, they fished the open sea and evaporated sea water to make salt. The Venetian economy quickly prospered, but the city was also keen to expand its commercial boundaries. Venice slowly began to take control of trade in the Adriatic Sea, suppressing pirates and establishing trading stations. Trading agreements with some of the most powerful states of the era guaranteed Venice independence and gave it important trading privileges.

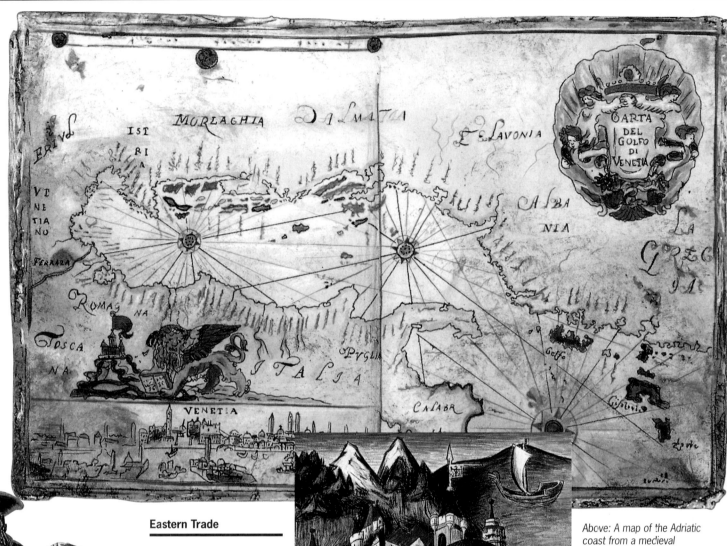

*The "Bailo," the Venetian ambassador of Constantinople.*

*Above: A map of the Adriatic coast from a medieval navigation manual. From the 9th century, Venice traded extensively in this area.*

*Left: The walled city of Constantinople.*

*Below: Early Venetian shipwrights are depicted in this stone relief in St. Mark's Basilica.*

## Eastern Trade

Commercial expansion began early in Venice. By the end of the 9th century, trade with the East had begun. Doge Pietro Orseolo II, who governed from 991–1008, organized a commercial agreement with Constantinople, which saw Venice receive the majority of Byzantine imports. Silk, spices, and precious metals arrived from the East, while slaves, salt, and wood were sent to Constantinople and the Levant from Torcello and the Rialto area. As the volume of trade increased, the Venetians redistributed the imported goods to other parts of Italy and their prosperity grew.

## The Crusades

Venice grew enormously rich from its trading links with the East. When the Crusaders began invading the Holy Land in the late 11th century, the Venetians saw an opportunity for trading expansion. They established themselves as one of the main suppliers to the Crusaders, and gained valuable trading rights in conquered cities such as Antioch and Tripoli.

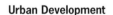

*The Crusades were launched by Pope Urban II in 1095. Crusaders besieged Antioch in 1098.*

## Urban Development

In the 9th and 10th centuries, only a cluster of small islands existed in the Rialto area. By the 11th century, however, a new commercial center had developed, and the Rialto gradually became the hub of the city. Workshops, businesses, and shops were established, and churches and new buildings were constructed throughout the city. Meanwhile Murano and the other islands remained densely populated, holding onto their own economic resources of fishing and salt production.

## The Trading City

Venice's prosperity during the medieval period was built on trade, but also on political deals. After the Venetian navy helped the Byzantine emperor Alexius Comnenus fight off the Normans in 1081, the emperor declared Venetian traders exempt from taxes throughout the empire. Medieval Venice was a cosmopolitan city, allowing foreigners to manage their businesses in freedom. Alongside Venetian merchants, it was not uncommon to find Turkish, German, and Arab traders.

*A 13th-century statue of a Moorish trader, with turban, on the Campo dei Mori in Cannaregio.*

**1100 – 1400**

**1128** Street lighting first appears in Venice.

**1171** Venice's six districts (sestieri) are established.

**1173** The first Rialto Bridge is built.

**13th century** Venice is the main naval power in the

## Economic Prosperity

The Crusades brought a huge increase in the amount of trade between west and east, and between north and south, and much of it passed through Venice. Here, everything was available — silks, ceramics, jewels, and spices from the east, gold from Africa, and grain, furs, and woolen cloth from northern Europe. Merchants prospered, as did bankers and moneylenders. Then, at the beginning of the 13th century, the Venetians raided Constantinople, their main rival in the Christian

Mediterranean, along with its rival Genoa.

**1204** Venetian navy raids Constantinople and returns with many precious art treasures.

**1295** Marco Polo returns from China.

**1325** The names of the

world. As well as carrying off many valuable artistic treasures, they forced the Byzantines to give up nearly half their empire. Venice fought hard for its prosperity.

city's noble families are written in the Libro d'Oro ("Golden Book").

**1340** Work begins on the Doge's Palace.

**1348–9** The Black Death strikes Venice.

*These four bronze horses were brought back to Venice from Constantinople after the Fourth Crusade (1202–04). They can still be seen in St. Mark's Basilica.*

*In medieval Venice, units of currency and rates of exchange were established. Gold ducats were first minted in Venice in 1284.*

# Medieval Venice

**P**erfectly positioned at the crossroads of Europe, Venice thrived as trade and commerce boomed during the Middle Ages. The city was at the heart of new technological and financial developments, such as the mastery of glassmaking and the exchange of hard currencies. Venice also absorbed a mix of new cultural influences, some of them a direct result of ruthless attacks on rival powers, such as Constantinople — attacks in which the formidable power of Venice's navy, built in the newly founded Arsenal, played a crucial role. The range of cultural influences was embodied in splendid new buildings, such as the Doge's Palace and the stunning Byzantine and Gothic palaces on the Grand Canal. But while some in medieval Venice were able to flaunt their wealth, others struggled to survive. When disasters such as the Black Death arrived, however, they struck rich and poor alike.

*A 14th-century glass lantern in the shape of a horse, from Murano.*

## Living in Medieval Venice

Medieval Venice was a wealthy, commercial city, teeming with foreign traders and merchants eager to develop new ideas, such as printing and banking. Elegant and elaborately decorated palaces were built throughout the city, many serving both as a home and warehouse for rich trading families. The wealth of the city was evident in its beautiful buildings and well-dressed nobility, but so too was its poverty and filth. Most streets in medieval Venice were unpaved and covered in the garbage that

Venetians threw out of their windows. This created dirt and disease, and when it rained or there was a high tide, the streets became quagmires of mud. The only system of street cleaning were the pigs, who fed on and destroyed large quantities of garbage. For this reason, many Venetian men and women wore high-heeled shoes to keep their clothes above the filth on the streets, or they moved around the city on horseback or by gondola.

*A Venetian noblewoman of the 13th century.*

*Counting out money in a medieval Venetian bank. The character Shylock in Shakespeare's play The Merchant of Venice, although a racial stereotype, is based on Jewish moneylenders working in medieval Venice.*

*Left: A sign for a medieval butcher's shop.*

## Mid-14th century

Painter Lorenzo Veneziano and others begin to combine the Gothic style with more traditional Byzantine artistic influences.

**1379–80** Venice is victorious in the War of Chioggia, defeating its arch rival, Genoa.

*Byzantine artworks, such as the Coronation of the Virgin by Paolo Veneziano (right), were intended to encourage religious devotion rather than being a faithful representation of reality.*

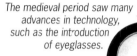

*The medieval period saw many advances in technology, such as the introduction of eyeglasses.*

## Medieval Venetian Art

Venice's close links with the Byzantine Empire were evident in Venetian art of the medieval period, with its emphasis on symmetry and love of gold decoration, together with the rather stiff, formal figures. These elements are all visible in the work of the first great Venetian painter, Paolo Veneziano (c.1290–c.1360), active in the mid-14th century. The unrelated Lorenzo Veneziano a generation later, introduced more Gothic elements, such as ornate decoration and flowing, sinuous figures.

## The Black Death

The terrible plague that ravaged Europe in the middle of the 14th century was spread by fleas that lived on one species of rat. During the terrible years of the Black Death, Venice's population was reduced from 160,000 to less than half that figure. It took nearly two centuries to reach its original size again.

*During the Black Death, medieval doctors covered themselves to avoid infection. The "beak" was filled with pungent herbs, to purify the air.*

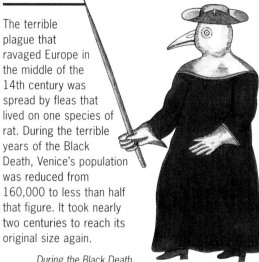

*Below: A 14th-century manuscript illustration of Venice showing Marco Polo setting out for China in 1271.*

## Marco Polo

In 1295, a Venetian called Marco Polo (1254–1324) returned to the city after an absence of 17 years. He claimed that for most of that time he had been a guest of Emperor Kublai Khan in China, and in 1298 he wrote an account of his experiences known as *The Travels of Marco Polo*. Unfortunately, many people did not believe some of his observations, especially as he did not even mention the Great Wall of China or the important role of tea drinking in Chinese life. Although known in history as a great explorer, he was probably simply an intrepid Venetian merchant.

commence li livres du graunt Caam qui parole de la graunt Ermenie et perse et des tartars et dynde. Et des graunz merveille qui ple monde sont.

## THE DOGE'S PALACE

**9th century** The Doge's Palace is first built as a fortified castle.

**1340** Work begins on the palace that visitors see today.

**1438** With the construction of the Porta della Carta, the palace is essentially complete.

**1483** Fire damages much of the palace.

**1485** Antonio Rizzo builds the Giants' Staircase.

**1565** Sansovino decorates the Giants' Staircase with statues of Mars and Neptune.

**1574, 1577** Two fires

destroy much of the interior of the palace, including many artworks.

**1600** Antonio Contino builds the Bridge of Sighs.

**1870s** A major restoration project begins.

**1924** The palace is opened to the public as a

museum.

**1970s** Restoration of the Porta della Carta.

### A Gothic Masterpiece

Most of the façade of this highly ornate palace is of patterned white and rose-colored marble, set over a gallery of lace-like tracery. The overall effect is extraordinarily light and delicate, and the building is

a masterpiece of Gothic architecture. The main entrance to the palace was the 15th-century Porta della Carta, leading to a courtyard with two magnificent stairways — the Golden Staircase and the Giants' Staircase. Completed during the 15th and 16th centuries,

the upper stories are finely decorated with Renaissance paintings and sculpture by artists such as Tintoretto, Veronese, and Rizzo.

*This sculpture of Doge Francesco Foscari (ruled 1423–57) kneeling before the Lion of Venice sits above the Porta della Carta.*

*Below: The election of the doge was by secret ballot. Each voter cast a colored wax counter into an urn like this.*

*In the late 14th century, the piazzetta in front of the Doge's Palace would have been a hive of activity, with people disembarking and goods being unloaded at the Molo ("quay").*

# The Doge's Palace

**B**uilding work on the Doge's Palace began in the 14th century and continued unabated for many years. The official residence of the doge, the palace also housed the institutions of the Venetian Republic and served as the center of political life. One of the most spectacular examples of Gothic architecture in the world, the palace was built to impress, and to show visitors the grandeur and wealth of the Venetian Republic. As Venice grew richer, the palace expanded, and although it suffered a number of fires in the early years, the city's wide-ranging trade connections are still reflected in the palace's architecture — Gothic and Byzantine with traces of Islamic style. The English writer John Ruskin, visiting in the mid-19th century, called it "the central building of the world."

### The Working Palace

The palace was not just a lavish home for the doge, though there were private apartments for him. It was also the heart of the city's government and administration. The Council of Ten met here, as well as the Senate and the Grand Council, made up of all the

city's nobles. It was also where legal trials were held, and where most offenders were imprisoned, until the new prison was built at the start of the 17th century.

*A view of the Doge's Palace by Luca Carlevaris (1665–1731) showing an official visit by the British ambassador in 1707.*

## The Doge of Venice

The doge was the head of the Venetian Republic (see pages 22–23) and was elected for life by the members of Venice's Grand Council of noblemen. Although he had considerable power, he was not able to make policy decisions on his own. He always had to win the approval of the Senate. Despite his privileges, the doge remained a servant of the Venetian Republic. He couldn't even leave the city unless accompanied by two or more of his councillors!

*The doge had a variety of ceremonial hats. This one was known as the "corno."*

*Giovanni Bellini's magnificent portrait of Doge Leonardo Loredan, painted shortly after his election in 1501.*

## The Bridge of Sighs

Built in the early 17th century to connect the law courts of the Doge's Palace with the new prisons, the Bridge of Sighs was not given this name until 200 years later. Prisoners being led off to jail would catch a final, fleeting glimpse of the lagoon and the island of San Giorgio, and could only sigh at the thought of the life that awaited them in jail.

*The Bridge of Sighs led prisoners to the new prisons, which were fairly comfortable by 17th century standards.*

# 15th Century

### Building Work

Prosperous Venetians were not embarrassed about flaunting their wealth, and many of the city's most splendid palaces were built in the 15th century. Previously a city built largely of wood and timber, in the early 1400s, stunning new brick buildings began to appear. One of these was the Ca' d'Oro (the "Golden House"), on the Grand Canal, built between 1421 and 1434 (see page 39). Designed by Giovanni Bon,

*The 15th-century Palazzo Contarini del Bovolo is famous for the spectacular tower containing its spiral staircase.*

one of a celebrated family of Venetian architects, it is in an extravagant late Gothic style. Towards the end of the century, the influence of the

*This 15th-century map of Venice is in the city's magnificent Marciana Library. Many of the churches and*

Renaissance began to appear, for example in the church of San Zaccaria and the church of the Frari.

*monasteries shown on it have been demolished over the centuries.*

### The Barovier Family

For centuries, the island of Murano (see pages 36–37) has been famous as a center of glassmaking. Among the leading exponents of the art in the

15th century were the Barovier family, who had three prosperous glass furnaces on Murano. Angelo Barovier is credited with creating the first complete transparent "crystal glass," around 1450.

*Left: This white glass, made by Giovanni Barovier in the late 15th century, was meant to imitate Chinese porcelain.*

*Right: This beautiful example of Venetian craftsmanship was designed to hold religious relics.*

**V**enice was at the height of its power in the 15th century. Its territories expanded west and north into mainland Italy, and its naval supremacy in the region was unrivaled. Within the city itself, building work boomed, and many new churches and monasteries were founded. Nevertheless, it was not a century of peace. Under the ambitious Doge Francesco Foscari, Venice was soon at war with its main Italian rival, Milan, while other cities grew increasingly suspicious and jealous of Venetian power. To the east, the Turks were a serious threat to Venice's economic power, while the discovery of America at the end of the century, and of a sea route to India, would eventually lead to Venice's decline as a commercial power.

*These 15th-century platform shoes had a practical purpose in a city where the streets were often under water!*

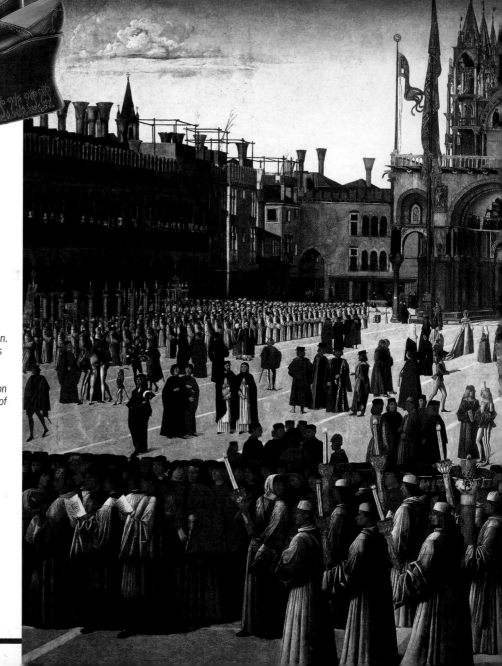

### Venetian Fashions

The wealth and power of Venice during the 15th century were reflected in its citizens' taste for lavish clothes. Colors were ravishing, and luxurious materials such as silk and velvet, sometimes with gold thread interwoven, were widely available. Venice dominated the European silk industry at this time, and constant changes in fashion helped keep business booming for cloth manufacturers. Venice's trading links with the East meant that weavers were always able to incorporate the latest exotic designs and motifs into their fabrics.

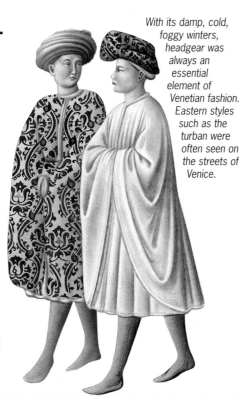

*With its damp, cold, foggy winters, headgear was always an essential element of Venetian fashion. Eastern styles such as the turban were often seen on the streets of Venice.*

## Masks

In 15th century Venice, the manufacture of masks, worn during the Carnival, was considered as important an art as glassmaking or lace production, and mask-makers had their own trade association. Many of the designs were based on characters in the popular theater, the *Commedia dell' Arte* (see page 25), such as the clown Harlequin.

*One of the most common types of mask was the volto, which only covered the top half of the face, allowing the wearer to eat and drink.*

# Venice

*Gentile Bellini's painting of A Procession in St Mark's Square (1496) captures the magnificence of the city during the late 15th century.*

## 1400 – 1499

## Artists' Venice

At the beginning of the 15th century, painters such as Gentile da Fabriano were working in a florid decorative style known as International Gothic. The middle part of the century saw the emergence of the great Bellini family of painters. Giovanni Bellini (c.1433–1516) painted religious pictures and was one of the finest portraitists of his time, while his brother Gentile (c.1429–1507) won a reputation as a fine painter of legends. Among their contemporaries was Vittore Carpaccio, born in Venice in around 1465, who also painted historical and mythical stories. Through artists such as these, Venetian painting won its reputation for bright, vivid colors, and a love of intricate detail.

*Vittore Carpaccio loved to pack his depictions of legends with details from everyday life. This scene is a detail from one of a series of nine paintings on The Life of St. Ursula, an early Christian martyr.*

**1403** A quarantine is imposed on newcomers to the city in an attempt to prevent recurrences of the Black Death.

**1423** Francesco Foscari becomes doge and embarks on war with Milan.

**1430** Giovanni Bellini is born in Venice.

**1437** The Ca' Foscari is built for the doge.

**1454** The Treaty of Lodi brings peace with Milan and other Italian states.

**1457** Doge Foscari is forced to abdicate by the Venetian Council.

**1468** Cardinal Bessarion donates over 1,000 manuscripts to the state library in Venice.

**1471** Doge Nicolò Tron has Venetian coins struck with his effigy, the only doge to do so.

**1499** Vasco da Gama discovers a sea route to India.

*Above: A 15th century view of St. Mark's Square and the Doge's Palace.*

## The Renaissance City

Magnificent art, architecture, and entertainment thrived during the Renaissance period. The Gothic style of the Middle Ages had left its mark on Venice, making it one of the most beautiful cities in Europe, and this was enriched during the Renaissance. Although a rather conservative city politically, it was culturally free and relaxed. It was this atmosphere that attracted the artists, poets, scholars, and musicians who would make Venice one of the most important cities in Renaissance times.

*Right: The Feast in the House of Levi by Paolo Veronese (1528–88) is a* splendid example of his contribution to Renaissance art in Venice.

## 1400 – 1599

**1424–27** The Doge's Palace is enlarged and is attached to the side of St. Mark's Basilica.

**1454** The Peace of Lodi, which gives the Italian state 50 years of stability, secures the artistic and cultural reawakening of Venice.

**1475–76** Antonello da Messina, a Sicilian painter, astounds Venetians with his Altarpiece in the medieval church of San Cassiano.

**1479** On the request of the Venetian government, Gentile Bellini goes to Constantinople as a painter to the sultan, Mehmed II.

# Renaissance

The Renaissance was the golden age of art in Venice. After Florence, the city was one of the great capitals of the Renaissance, attracting artists to its rich, splendid way of life and easy-going atmosphere. Links with the East, great trading success, and a cosmopolitan lifestyle saw Venice make its mark in the Renaissance world, and through the 16th century it was probably Europe's most influential cultural center. Dazzling Renaissance palaces were built along the Grand Canal, the Venetian State employed some of the most important painters of the time, and fashion and music reached new heights. It was an age of unrivaled glory for the city.

## Commerical Riches

For years Venice had dominated the Mediterranean and controlled trade with the East. For Venetian merchants and traders, no transaction was worthless. The city had commercial dealings with the princes of North Africa, Syria, and Egypt, the Muslim countries at the head of the caravan routes that transported spices, colored pigments, cloth, and precious stones from India and China. The Venetian Republic also had a monopoly over alum, extracted from the mines of Asia Minor, and in great demand in the dye-works of Europe for fixing colors to cloth. Such commercial richness meant that Venice was a fabulously wealthy city at the beginning of the Renaissance period. It was during this time that Venetian glassblowers rediscovered the techniques for making fine glassware, a trade which by the 17th century was a thriving industry on the island of Murano.

*A 16th century Venetian chair made of walnut.*

*Venice and its lagoon in a fresco by Ignazio Danti (1536–86).*

**1490** Aldus Manutius sets up his Aldine Press in Venice. The colophon of the Aldine Press showed an anchor and dolphin (right).

**Early 1500s** Over 16,000 prostitutes working in Venice.

**1501** The 20-year rule of Doge Leonardo Loredan, the great diplomat, begins.

**1518** Titian's painting *The Assumption* is hung in the church of the Frari. Tintoretto is born in Venice.

**1522** The Ottomans drive the Venetians out of the Eastern Mediterranean.

**1527** The Ospedaletto, a shelter for cripples, the old, and poor women, is created.

**Mid 1500s** First reviews of the *Commedia dell' Arte*.

**1545** Ca' Grande is designed for the Cornaro family, one of the richest families in Venice.

**1563** The population of Venice is nearly 170,000.

**1576** Titian dies in Venice and Veronese becomes the official painter of the Republic.

### Life in Renaissance Venice

For the wealthy, of which there were many, life in Venice during the Renaissance period was luxurious, and was often reflected in their elaborate wardrobes. Men wore large, pleated capes decorated with silk and velvet brocade over embroidered tights, while women's gowns were often adorned with bold jewelry. Veronese's *Feast in the House of Levi* (left), painted in 1573, reflects the splendor and vitality of life in Venetian society during the Renaissance.

### Renaissance Architecture

Venice was highly influenced by the ideals of Renaissance architecture. Sumptuous new facades, which were characterized by superimposed porticoes, balconies, and arched windows, appeared during this period. Building renovations took place throughout much of the city, and along the Grand Canal several Renaissance palaces were constructed, including the Palazzo Vendramin, built in the early 16th century by chief architect Mauro Coducci (1440–1504).

*Above: The Palazzo Vendramin today houses the winter quarters of the municipal casino. The composer Richard Wagner died here in 1883.*

*Below: 16th-century musicians in St. Mark's Square during the Doge's Palm Sunday procession.*

# Splendor

### Renaissance Art

The Renaissance was a time of brilliance and vitality in art. Ancient Greek and Roman models were the basis of new creations, and there was a passion for the portrayal of the human body and nature in art. In Venice, artists such as Titian and Veronese contributed greatly to Renaissance art. One of the most important figures of the High Renaissance, Titian became official state painter in 1517, while Veronese adorned the Doge's Palace with some of its most stunning works of art.

*Tiziano Vecellio (1490–1576), known at Titian, was a master Renaissance painter of the Venetian school.*

*Sacred Love and Profane Love (below) painted by Titian between 1516 and 1518. In this work, he established the basic rule of depicting the beauty of the human figure, an essential ingredient of the Renaissance period.*

*A detail from Titian's Diana and Aceteon. The return of themes from classical mythology was also a characteristic of Renaissance art.*

### Making Music

The Renaissance also sparked dramatic changes in music, as it became an important element of cultural life and society. One of the most popular and widely diffused musical instruments of the Renaissance period was the lute. In Venice, the organ was enjoyed and flocks of music lovers gathered in St. Mark's Basilica to listen to concerts by great music masters. Wind instruments such as cornets, trumpets, flutes, bassoons, and oboes were also played at society balls, marches, and processions.

The name "Arsenal" comes from the Arabic word *darsina'a*, meaning "workshop." In its heyday in the mid-16th century, the Arsenal was the ultimate symbol of Venice's power. It was here that the ships and boats for Venetian merchants and the naval fleet, on which the city's wealth and independence rested, were built. Highly efficient, the Arsenal has been called the first modern factory. As such, it was also an obvious target when the city was occupied by Napoleon Bonaparte's troops at the end of the 18th century. By the 20th century, when Venice was no longer a political and naval power, parts of the Arsenal were used as exhibition centers for the Biennale art exhibition.

## THE ARSENAL

**1104** Probable founding of the Arsenal.

**1306** The poet Dante visits Venice and is so impressed by the Arsenal that he describes it in his poem, *The Divine Comedy*.

**1460** The main gateway of the Arsenal is built.

**1473** Faced with the growing power of the Spanish and the Turks, the Venetian Senate decides to build a new arsenal, the "Arsenale Novissimo," as an extension to the original shipyard.

**c. 1560** The Arsenal is at the height of its powers, employing as many as 16,000 workers, about 10% of Venice's population.

**17th century** The Arsenal becomes less active as Venice declines as a commercial power.

**1797** Napoleon's troops capture Venice and set fire to the Arsenal.

### The "Novissimo"

The building of the "Arsenale Novissimo" was a key factor in ensuring the naval supremacy of Venice in the late 15th and 16th centuries. There had probably never been production on such a scale, and the size of some of the buildings was, for the time, extraordinary. The building known as La Tana, for example, which was used for ropemaking, was about 1,020 feet (310 m) long and 75 feet (22 m) wide.

# The Arsenal

*This drawing by the artist Raphael (1483–1520) shows a typical Venetian galley from around 1500.*

*In the mid-16th century, the workers in the Arsenal could construct and equip a ship a day.*

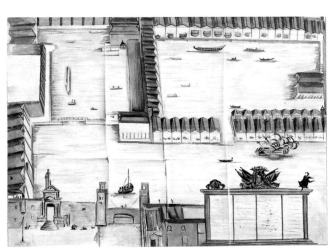

*Plan of the Arsenal in the 17th century, by Antonio di Natale.*

### The First Arsenal

The exact date of the founding of the Arsenal is unknown, although some sources give 1104. By the early 13th century, a basic form of Arsenal existed, in the form of a dockyard where private contractors could make repairs to ships' hulls and sell items such as rigging and oars. It was not until the early 14th century that a state monopoly was established to build ships, although there were still thousands of small private companies engaged in every aspect of ship maintenance.

*Visitors to the city in the 16th century were often as impressed by the efficiency of the Arsenal as they were by the grandeur of St. Mark's Square.*

### Boatbuilding

In the mid-16th century, the Arsenal resembled something like a modern-day industrial assembly line, with ships being built at incredible speed. The hulls were assembled in the New Arsenal and were then fitted out in the Old Arsenal with masts, sails, oars, weapons, and provisions. So smooth was this process that, according to one story, in 1574, during a state visit by the French King Henri III, a fully seaworthy ship was built in the time it took the king to be treated to a lavish banquet.

**1917** Dockyards dismantled.

**2003** The future of the Arsenal is under review.

## The Workers

Most of the workers, known as the *arsenalotti*, were specialized tradesmen, such as carpenters, ropemakers, or caulkers (producing the pitch used to make the ships' hulls watertight), and they were well paid by the standards of the time. In the winter the typical working day lasted only six hours,

but in the summer they worked a 12-hour day. All work had to be done during daylight — artificial lighting was prohibited because of the risk of fire. Most of the workers lived in the district of San Pietro di Castello. So respected were the Arsenal workers that an élite group of them was chosen to form the doge's honor guard, accompanying him on state occasions in the *Bucintoro*.

*The arsenalotti also served as Venice's firefighters.*

*Lions like this stand guard outside the gates of the Arsenal.*

## The *Bucintoro*

The doge's galley, known as the *Bucintoro*, was constructed with particular pride. It was used for elaborate state occasions, such as receiving important guests on state visits, and for the annual ceremony of the doge's "marriage with the sea" (see page 23).

The first *Bucintoro* was probably built as early as 1311. The last one was built in 1729 — a scale model is now preserved in the city's Naval Museum.

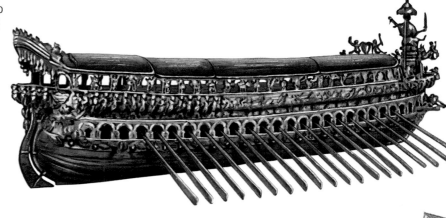

*The Bucintoro was capable of carrying up to 200 men and, many say, resembled a gilded dragon with the Lion of St. Mark on its prow.*

## The Arsenal Today

Part of the Arsenal is used today by the Italian navy for storage and repairs, but every two years the huge La Tana building is the venue for the Venice Biennale (see page 34), a highly prestigious exhibition of contemporary art from around the world. There are now plans to convert part of the Arsenal into a cultural center.

*This sculpture of a young boy by Ron Mueck was displayed in the Arsenal during the 49th Venice Biennale in 2001.*

## STREETS AND SQUARES

**9th century** The church of St. Cassiano is built in Campo San Cassiano.

**12th century** St. Mark's Square is first laid out.

**15th century** Campo San Polo is the scene of spectacular balls, ceremonies, and bull-baiting.

**1592** Campo San Zanipolo is paved by Dominican friars.

**1676** The first paved streets are completed.

**18th century** Gabriele Bella paints the games and cruel sports played in Venice's *campi*.

**1806–16** The Public

Gardens are laid out.

**1871–2** The Austrians build the Strada Nuova, running from the station to the Rialto Bridge.

**1883** A statue of Carlo Goldoni is erected in Campo San Bartolomeo.

**1893** Ferdinando Ongania

publishes his book 'Calli e Canali di Venezia.'

**1907** A new fish market is built near the Rialto.

**1966** Terrible flooding in many streets and squares of the city.

**W**hile Venice's canals are a world-famous means of getting about the city, its network of narrow, winding streets (*calli*) and not-so-square squares (*campi*) are an equally important part of daily life. Venice's labyrinth of streets arose early in the city's history, as almost every available piece of land was used to build houses, churches, and shops. Built on hundreds of small islands, Venice is unique in the modern world for having no motor traffic. Its streets and alleyways, leading onto *campi* and the smaller *campielli*, are far too narrow for cars to pass through, meaning the city is best explored on foot.

*This beautiful well illustrates how, in Venice, even the essentials of daily life are seen as an opportunity for artistic design.*

# Streets and

**Water and Wells**

In medieval and Renaissance times, sanitary conditions in Venice were, by modern standards, unsatisfactory. There was no proper garbage collection or drainage, and people would often simply throw refuse (of all sorts!) out of the windows or into the canals. Many of the squares, or *campi*, had a well — in some cases there might be as many as four — in which rainwater would collect. This provided most people's drinking water, although some families were fortunate enough to have

# CAMPO S.BARTOLOMEO

*Most of Venice's squares contain a church, and often the square will take its name from the church.*

their own private well. Another possibility was to buy water from one of the water-sellers who brought in clean water from outside the city, or to collect water from one of the public fountains.

# Squares

## Street Entertainment

In the 17th and 18th centuries, in particular, Venice had a reputation for having the liveliest street life in Europe. The government thought that providing regular games would encourage a feeling of patriotism and contentment. Ice-skating was a popular sport during cold winters, while wheelbarrow-racing, in which the city's street cleaners regularly competed, was also enjoyed. Other entertainments were more gruesome, such as bear-baiting or goose-chasing. There were also many religious festivals and the extravagant celebrations to mark the election of a new doge. The highlight of the year, though, was — and still is — the Carnival (see pages 24–25).

*An aerial view of Venice showing its dense network of streets, squares, and canals.*

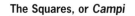

*This street entertainer is dressed as Harlequin, a character from the Commedia dell' Arte, an early form of popular theater in Italy.*

## Statues

Among the best-known monuments in Venice is the bronze statue of Bartolomeo Colleoni. This masterpiece of Renaissance sculpture was designed by the artist Andrea del Verrocchio. At his death, Colleoni, who had amassed a considerable fortune, left all his possessions to the Venetian Republic on condition that they erect a statue of him in St. Mark's Square. However, a law forbidding the building of any monuments in the square put a stop to this, and instead the Campo San Zanipolo was chosen.

*Bartolomeo Colleoni was one of the Venetian Republic's most feared military leaders of the 15th century.*

## A Photographic Record

At the end of the 19th century, the Venetian photographer Ferdinando Ongania published two important books documenting daily life in Venice — *Calli e Canali in Venezia* ("Streets and Canals of Venice") and *Isole della Laguna* ("Islands of the Lagoon"). Both books are compilations of photographs of every aspect of daily life in the city, providing a fascinating and unique historical document.

*Ferdinando Ongania caught some of the less picturesque aspects of 19th century Venetian life.*

*In the 18th century, Venice's streets were noisy, busy places. In this painting by Gabriele Bella we see two masked Venetians passing by a poor fruit seller.*

## The Streets, or *Calli*

While in most parts of Italy a street is known as a *via* or *strada*, in Venice the most common word for a street is *calle* (plural, *calli*). However, Venetians have a huge variety of words for different types of street. A *riva* is a quayside, and a *fondamento* is a street running along the side of a canal, while a very short street might be a *ramo*, and a little covered alleyway is a *sottoportego*. Many of the streets are named for the products traditionally traded in them, such as the "Street of the Spice Dealer" or the "Street of the Wine Merchant." Others reflect the cosmopolitan city that Venice once was — for example, *Calli dei Tedeschi* ("Street of the Germans").

*The vegetable and pumpkin-seller was a familiar sight on the streets of 18th century Venice.*

## Street Life

Venice has always been a thriving commercial center, its streets thronging with a wide variety of tradesmen plying their wares. When Venice first became a popular tourist venue in the 18th century, many visitors commented on some of the more exotic merchandise on sale, such as the wide variety of sweetmeats, or *bussolai*. A popular landmark was the Erberia, the market near the Rialto Bridge, where flowers, fruit, and vegetables were sold, and which still exists today.

*The city's first fish market opened in the 14th century.*

## The Squares, or *Campi*

There is only one piazza in Venice — the Piazza San Marco, or St. Mark's Square (see pages 28–29). All the other main squares of the city are known as *campi*, or *campiello* (small squares). Only a few of the city's squares are in fact square — many are rectangular and some are completely irregular, or even L-shaped.

*Venice's smaller squares are peaceful places, away from the bustle of everyday life.*

Paul IV (1476–1559) was the first pope of the Counter-Reformation, a period when the Catholic Church tried to reassert its authority after the rise of Protestantism in northern Europe.

### The Bull of 1555

On July 12, 1555, Pope Paul IV issued a bull, or decree, approving the establishment of the Ghetto. The bull, entitled "Cum Nimis Absurdum," stated that Jews should not live alongside Christians, but should be confined to their own specific areas.

*The decree that effectively sanctioned the Ghetto was issued just two months after Paul IV was elected Pope.*

# THE GHETTO

### The Jewish Community

Venice's Jewish community comprised groups from all over Europe. As early as the 14th century, Jewish merchants played a significant role in the city's economic life. The first substantial group of Jewish settlers, however, arrived in the 1490s from Spain and Portugal. A second group arrived in the early 1500s, fleeing persecution in northern and eastern Europe. With anti-Semitism prevalent in Europe at this time, the Ghetto in Venice was intended partly to guarantee the safety of the city's Jewish residents.

**Early 1300s** Jewish merchants settle in Venice.

**1381** Jews are officially authorized to live in the city on a renewable temporary license or *condotta*.

**1500s** Venice's first synagogues are built.

**1516** The New Ghetto is demarcated as a specifically Jewish area.

**1541** The Jewish quarter of Venice is enlarged to include the Old Ghetto.

**17th century** Population of the Ghetto is about 5,000.

**1633** The "Ghetto Novissimo" is added.

**1797** Napoleon abolishes the Ghetto, but many Jews continue to live there.

**1943–5** Transportation of Jews from Venice to death camps in Nazi Germany.

**2003** Jewish population of Venice estimated at around 600.

*There is often a reading from the Torah, the Hebrew Bible, in Jewish synagogues.*

# The Ghetto

For much of history, the Jewish people in Europe suffered persecution for having a religion and culture different from the majority. Between the 13th and 15th centuries, many Jews were expelled from parts of western Europe, and were forced to find new homes elsewhere. In the late 1400s, many Jewish people arrived in Venice after being thrown out of Spain and Portugal, and soon established businesses in the city. When the Venice Ghetto (in Venetian dialect, *geto*) was set up in 1516, however, they once again faced discrimination. The Ghetto continued to exist until 1797. Today, with its beautiful synagogues and Jewish museum, it serves as a spiritual focus for the city's Jewish residents and visitors.

*Part of the Venetian Ghetto in the 1960s.*

*Inside a Jewish apothecary, or chemist's shop*

### Ghetto Life

The inhabitants of the Ghetto (with the exception of doctors) were not allowed out of the area between sunset and sunrise. At night the gates of the Ghetto were locked and guarded by Christian watchmen. During the day, Jews were allowed out, but they had to wear a badge to identify themselves. Within the Ghetto, they were left to organize their own affairs, with butchers and bakers able to work according to the Jewish faith. It was a vibrant, cosmopolitan community (Venetian Jews came from all over the world), with an inn, a hospital, numerous bookstores, an academy of music, and a theater.

### The Jewish Cemetery

Abandoned in the 18th century, the Jewish cemetery on the Lido di Venezia (about 30 minutes from the Ghetto by boat) is sometimes said to be the oldest graveyard in Europe. It was founded in 1386, on land that had previously been a vineyard belonging to the Benedictine monastery of San Nicolò di Mira. Bodies were transported by a cortège of funeral gondolas belonging to the *Hevrat Ghemilut Hassad'm*, the Jewish burial society.

*Jews were buried in different areas of the cemetery, depending on their nationality.*

## Jews and Venetians

Although Venice was considered religiously tolerant toward Jews compared to other parts of Europe in the early 16th century, there were times of friction and many Venetians were anti-Semitic. During the Carnival period, a formal proclamation forbidding attacks on Jews was often issued.

*Some of the masks worn by Venetians at Carnival time originated as cruel caricatures of Jewish features.*

## The Synagogues

The synagogues of Venice were known as "schole" or "schools," and each served a different part of the Jewish community. The first of these, the *Schola Grande Tedesca*, or "Great German School," was established in 1528 in the Campo del Ghetto Nuovo, by Jews who had fled from Germany. At one time there were nine synagogues in the Ghetto, most of them discreetly situated on the upper floor of a building.

*Left: A ketoubah, or Jewish marriage contract, from the Jewish museum.*

*The Schola Spagnola is perhaps the most splendid Jewish monument in Venice.*

## Building in the Ghetto

Since they were confined to a limited space, the Jews of the Ghetto were forced to build upward as the community expanded. The houses became the tallest in Venice, virtual skyscrapers, sometimes with as many as nine storeys.

*Jews living in the Ghetto were cut off from the rest of Venice by wide canals and two water gates.*

## Emancipation

The late 18th century was a time when human rights was of great concern throughout Europe, and more liberal attitudes towards Jews and other minorities took hold. Despite this, in 1775, Pope Pius VI issued an edict that led to further restrictions on Jewish communities all over Europe. For Venice, the end of the 18th century saw its capture by the French leader Napoleon, who ordered an end to the isolation of the Jewish population. Venetian Jews, however, remained in confinement even under Austrian rule (1798–1866), although unofficially. When Venice became part of Italy in 1866, the Jewish residents were granted equal status in law by Victor Emmanuel II, and were finally free to lead normal lives in the city.

*The papal edict of 1775 tried to stem the tide of liberalism.*

## Traditions and Festivals

In order to retain their sense of identity as a community, the inhabitants of the Ghetto observed all the Jewish traditions. During the spring festival of Purim, for example, there were masks and street dancing, just as in the rest of Venice at Carnival time.

*During Sukkot, Jews build a temporary shelter known as a sukkah, to commemorate the journey to the Promised Land. This sukkah is being transported by gondola.*

## The Ghetto Today

Today, the Jewish population of Venice is probably only around 600, of whom only a few live in the Ghetto. Nevertheless, the Ghetto remains the spiritual home of the city's Jewish community, with a museum, library, and synagogues. In the northern corner of the Campo del Ghetto Nuovo are seven relief sculptures commemorating the victims of the Holocaust.

*The Campo del Ghetto Nuovo as it looks today.*

**1000 – 1797**

**1000** Venetian navy defeats pirates in the Adriatic.

**1255** Creation of the Venetian Senate.

**1297** Membership of the Grand Council is limited to members of noble families.

**1310** The Council of Ten

is set up.

**1404** The Venetian Republic takes control away from the Milanese in the Veneto area, thus becoming stronger on the mainland.

**1416** After defeating the Turks at the Battle of Gallipoli, Venice is at the height of its powers.

**1453** The fall of Constantinople into Muslim hands weakens Venetian power in the East.

**1489** Venice captures Cyprus.

**1500s** Grand Council numbers over 2,000.

**1508** Pope Julius II

organizes the League of Cambrai, an alliance of all Venice's enemies.

**1571** Battle of Lepanto.

**1630** Plague strikes again in Venice.

**1797** Defeat of the Republic by Napoleon's troops.

**Venetian Supremacy**

By the beginning of the 16th century, Venice had colonized much of northeast Italy, while controlling the waters of the Mediterranean as well. This made it an unrivaled trading center. While the Venetian

## Queen of Cyprus

In 1472, the Venetian noblewoman Caterina Cornaro married King James II of Cyprus. He died a year later in mysterious circumstances, and in 1474 their son also died, leaving Caterina as the island's queen. In 1489, the Republic forced her to abdicate and Cyprus was absorbed into the Venetian empire.

*After her abdication, Caterina Cornaro (1454–1510) lived out the rest of her life in the Italian town of Asolo.*

*A view of 16th century Venice. Venice's territories were divided into terra firma, lands within mainland Italy, and the stato da mar, its colonies in the eastern Mediterranean.*

# Rise and Fall of

The Venetians referred to their Republic as *La Serenissima* ("the most serene"), believing it supreme over every other nation. From the beginning of the 14th century to the end of the 16th, this was more or less true. Venice dominated the Mediterranean, foreign trade prospered, and its solid system of government ruled over a cultured and dynamic society. Its wealth and power were manifest in the magnificent public buildings and palaces built throughout the city, and its inhabitants declared themselves "Venetians first, Christians afterward." The city was to be envied. An economic crisis and another bout of plague in the early 17th century, however, saw the start of decline for the Venetian Republic, a process which continued unabated until its defeat at the end of the 1700s.

Republic was hardly a democracy by today's standards, the interests of the Republic always came first and no individual or group was above the law. By the end of the 17th century, its power was starting to wane as new trade routes opened up to America and Asia.

*Right: Sebastiano Venier commanded the Venetian fleet at the Battle of Lepanto (1571), and later became Doge of Venice, ruling from 1577 to 1578.*

# the Republic

## Venetian Government

Throughout Europe, the Venetian government was known for its stability and strong political institutions. The mainstay of the Republic was the Grand Council (*Maggior Consiglio*), which represented the whole of the city and passed laws. Its members were all noblemen, who were obliged to serve, and numbered several thousand by the 16th century. The Senate, created in 1255, debated policy and made recommendations to the Grand Council, which could approve or reject them.

*Members of the Senate were chosen from among the members of the Grand Council and served for a year. The Grand Council (above) was painted by Gabriele Bella (1730–82), a minor Venetian artist who chronicled daily life in the Serene Republic.*

*Venetians could post accusations against their neighbors through the bocca del leone or "lion's mouth," in the Council of Ten's meeting room in the Doge's Palace.*

## Council of Ten

Venice's Council of Ten was originally set up as a provisional measure to ensure the internal security of the Republic. In 1334, however, it became a permanent feature of the Venetian constitution. Anyone thought to be a threat to the state would be judged by the Council behind closed doors in its meeting room in the Doge's Palace, and might be tortured or imprisoned. With 16 members — ten Senators and the Doge's six "wise men," the Council gave the Venetian Republic a reputation for ruthlessness and secrecy.

*Below: The painter Andrea Vicentino (1539–1614) captured the spectacle of a state visit by King Henri III of France in 1574.*

## Military Victories

Venice's power and wealth did not necessarily mean a life of security and ease for its citizens. In fact, keeping hold of such a vast empire meant that the Republic was in an almost constant state of war. On October 7, 1571, at the Battle of Lepanto, off the coast of Greece, Venice played a major part in a massive victory for the united Christian forces over the Turks. More than half of their 214 warships were built in the Arsenal.

*The Doge's Palace houses a collection of weapons and armor, including this canon, from Venice's golden age.*

*Right: On state occasions, the doge was accompanied by his own chaplain, called the Primicero.*

*Below: This hatch-cover comes from the last Bucintoro to be built, by Antonio Corradini in 1729.*

## Official Ceremonies

The citizens of Venice enjoyed a range of festivals and ceremonies. As well as the traditional Christian feast days, there were special Venetian holidays, such as the Festival of La Salute, on November 21 (to thank the Virgin for her intervention against the plague in 1630), and the Procession to the convent of Santa Zaccaria, held on Easter Monday. The Venetian Republic also played host to many foreign heads of state.

## Ascension Day

One religious festival of special significance for the Venetians was Ascension Day. On that day in the year 1000 a fleet under Doge Pietro Orseolo II set sail to defeat pirates in the Adriatic Sea. On his return, the Senate ordered a special celebration, a symbolic "marriage with the sea." This became an annual event, celebrating Venice's unique relationship with the sea. The doge, dressed in gold and ermine, would sail into the lagoon on a special barge called the *Bucintoro* (see page 17) and throw a gold ring into the water. A version of the ceremony still takes place today.

*This meticulously detailed painting by the 18th-century artist Canaletto shows preparations for the "marriage with the sea."*

## Guilds and Industry

Between the 14th and 16th centuries, Venice was an important manufacturing center for products such as textiles, soap, and sugar.

Groups of workers — including foreigners based in the city — were allowed to form trade guilds known as *arti*. The *Arte della Seta*, for example, was the guild of silk workers.

*A guild emblem from Venice's Museo Correr.*

Carnevale, or Carnival, is Venice's largest festival. It takes place each spring in the period between Epiphany (January 6) and Mardi Gras (Fat Tuesday), the day before Lent begins. The festival's name derives from the Latin words *carne vale*, meaning "farewell to meat." No meat is eaten during the 40 days of Lent. The main focus of the Venetian Carnival are the final ten days before Lent, when thousands of masked and costumed revelers invade the city's streets and squares. Carnevale was outlawed at the fall of the Republic in 1797 but revived in the 1970s. Nowadays about 500,000 tourists take part in the festivities.

## Carnival Masks

Carnival revelers wear extravagant costumes, including ornate masks. Masqueraders traditionally address one another during the season as *Signor Maschera* ("Mister Mask"). Venetians have always been fond of disguise, as a way of indulging in illegal activities such as gambling or fighting duels. The wearing of costumes to disguise the wearer's identity has always been a central part of the Venice Carnival festivities, allowing revelers the opportunity to poke fun at authority figures. So great was the popularity of concealing one's identity that in the 17th century, the Senate thought it a danger to public safety and morality. Some of the most common masks are based on characters from the *Commedia dell' Arte*, but others are based on social observation, such as the *maschera nobile*, the nobleman's mask. The top half of the face is hidden

### CARNEVALE

**11th century** The first Carnival celebrations recorded in Venice.

**15th century** A guild of mask-makers is officially recognized.

**1608** The wearing of masks is outlawed, except during Carnival.

*During Carnival, the Campo San Maurizio is the venue for demonstrations of mask-making. Traditionally, most masks were made of leather or papier mâché.*

# Carnevale

## Carnival Origins

Carnevale has been celebrated in the Venice region since the 11th century. Its origins may lie in the ancient celebrations of the winter solstice, combined with Christian festivals — it originally began on December 26, the day after Christmas. Local fraternities known as *Compagnie della Calza*, some of which still exist, were responsible for organizing the main festivities in medieval times. The heyday of the

Carnival, however, was during the 18th century, when the city became particularly devoted to high living. Carnival at this time began with a series of balls in St. Mark's Square and the city's other large squares. Celebrations would continue throughout the season, with street vendors earning a handsome living, particularly those selling the traditional *fritole* or fritters. On the last day of the Carnival, an effigy of an unpopular figure would be burnt in the square.

*A group of glamorous revelers pose for the camera.*

*A Venetian man dressed for Carnival in the 1580s.*

centuries, but it was only at the end of the 1970s that the festival was revived in all its glory. The idea originally came from a group of non-Venetians, but the city authorities immediately took it up with great enthusiasm. One of the traditional rituals that has been revived is the opening ceremony, "the flight of the *colombina*," when a model of a dove on a piece of cable "flies" from the campanile across St. Mark's Square to the Doge's Palace. Today's Carnival is a mixture of official and "alternative" events.

*This white mask is a variant on the traditional* volto.

*This illustration shows Carnival revelers shocking the locals in St. Mark's Square in the 1500s.*

## Reviving the Carnival

When Napoleon captured Venice at the end of the 18th century, he outlawed the Carnival celebrations. There were attempts to revive the Carnival during the 19th and early 20th

**1645** An English visitor, John Evelyn, describes the Carnival as "folly and madness."

**1751** The highlight of the Carnival is a rhinoceros, put on public display.

**1797** Carnival is outlawed.

**1979** The revival in the

popularity of the Carnival begins, though it is limited to the ten days before Shrove Tuesday.

**1997** The Carnival takes as its theme the end of the Republic 200 years earlier.

**2000** An estimated 500,000 people visit Venice during the Carnival.

*The character of Pantalone is easy to recognize, with his bristling moustache and baggy trousers, in this painting (right) of the Venice Carnival during the 18th century by Giuseppe Ponga.*

### Commedia dell' Arte

The *Commedia dell' Arte* ("comedy of art") was a form of theater that developed in Italy during the 16th century. It was a mixture of improvised drama and circus spectacle, with not just actors but acrobats, musicians,

and all sorts of showmen demonstrating their skills. The *Commedia dell' Arte* was also an influence on Venice's most eminent playwright, Carlo Goldoni (1707–93), who satirized the daily life of Venice and its people in his plays. The form soon spread to other countries, such as France, where it developed into mime, and England, where the clown Pulcinella became Mr Punch in the puppet play, *Punch and Judy*.

behind the white mask called a *volto*, typically worn with a black silk hood called a *bautà*, under an enormous cloak, the *tabarro*, topped off by a three-cornered hat. However, there has always been plenty of scope for

inventing *fantasie*, or "fantasy masks," sometimes mocking Venice's enemies, or political figures.

## Ridotti

Particularly popular in the 18th century were the *ridotti* (gambling parlors), houses dedicated to witty conversation, gambling, and other forms of pleasure. The first *ridotto* opened in 1638 in the Palazzo Dandolo, but by the 18th century there were more than 100 of them. Toward the end of the century, all the *ridotti* were closed down, following the bankruptcy of many Venetian families. Cafés and *casini*, gentlemen's clubs, however, continued to prosper.

*Francesco Guardi, one of the most famous painters of 18th century Venice, painted The*

*Ridotto, where visitors wore masks to conceal their identity. Right: Venetian playing cards.*

**1700 – 1799**

**1703** Vivaldi begins work as violin master at the church of La Pietà.

**1718** Turks capture Venetian territories in the Aegean Sea, signaling the decline of Venice as a major military power.

**1725** Vivaldi composes *The Four Seasons*.

**1748** The Palazzo Grassi is built, the last of the great houses on the Grand Canal.

**1755** Casanova escapes from the Doge's Palace.

**1756** Canaletto returns to Venice from London.

**1767** Women are banned from cafés.

**1774** Closing of the state *ridotto*.

**1789** An English visitor, Hester Thrale, describes life in Venice as "subservient to the services of pleasure."

**1792** La Fenice opens.

**1797** The last doge of Venice abdicates.

## Theatrical Venice

The theater was a popular pastime in the 18th century. In 1770, the city had about 15 playhouses. In 1774, the most prestigious of these, the San Benedetto, burnt down. While it was being rebuilt, the theater's managers fell out with the owners and decided to open their own theater, La Fenice ("The Phoenix"). Venice's leading playwright at the time was Carlo Goldoni, who wrote plays for the theater. He is considered the great reformer of Italian comedy.

## Canaletto

The 18th century saw the emergence of one of Venice's most popular painters, Giovanni Antonio Canal, known as Canaletto (1697–1768). Born near the Rialto into a noble Venetian family, Canaletto quickly acquired a reputation for his beautiful and highly detailed views of the city. By 1730, these were in high demand from wealthy visitors wanting souvenirs of the city. Despite a short period in England, Canaletto's greatest work was produced in Venice.

*Since the majority of Canaletto's views of Venice were painted for foreign visitors, most of them now hang in collections in other countries. Below: St. Mark's Square by Canaletto.*

# 18th Century

In the 18th century, Venice, no longer a major political force, became a city devoted to pleasure. There was an explosion of creative activity, especially in music and the theater, but also in painting and craft. Yet the arts were not the only form of entertainment available to wealthy Venetians, happy to while away their time in the elegant coffee houses that began to appear around the city, to gamble away their fortunes in *ridotti*, and to seek out the company of obliging courtesans. The city was also a magnet for foreign visitors, and British aristocrats made the city a staging post on their "Grand Tour" of the great sights of Europe. While they all marveled at the city's artistic treasures, many were also shocked by the squalid conditions in which some of the city's inhabitants lived.

*San Benedetto Theater in 1782. Well-to-do families would buy a subscription for a whole season to a box at the San Benedetto.*

*Plays were performed to all levels of society at La Fenice.*

GRAN TEATRO LA FENICE

# Venice

## Casanova and Courtesans

Giovanni Giacomo Casanova (1725–98) is one of the most colorful figures of 18th century Venice. The son of an actor, he began training as a priest but was expelled from the seminary. He then worked as musician, writer, soldier, gambler, diplomat, and spy, visiting France, Germany, Bohemia, Russia, Spain, and England, befriending poets, philosophers, and aristocrats. He was most famous, though, for the romantic escapades recounted, and likely exaggerated, in his *Memoirs*. Many of these involve liaisons with the city's courtesans — ladies of pleasure who frequented the *ridotti*. Casanova's loose living epitomized Venetian decadence of the 18th century.

*Casanova was imprisoned in the Doge's Palace for "impiety and licentiousness," but escaped in 1755.*

*The church of San Geremia was built in the mid-18th century by Carlo Corbellini. It now houses the remains of the early Christian martyr St. Lucy, and its bell tower is one of the oldest in the city.*

## Fashion

In the 18th century, Venice was an extremely fashion-conscious city, with tastes influenced by Paris, then the capital of the fashion world. Brightly colored clothes were widely admired, with luxurious materials such as silk particularly popular. The wealthy spent huge amounts of money on clothing and jewelry. Men wore wigs, while women favored increasingly extravagant hair-dos. For a woman, a beauty spot was also a highly desirable feature.

*These woman's shoes, from the 1760s, are made of silk, interwoven with gold and silver thread. Heels were much lower in the 18th century.*

*In a society that took its leisure seriously, dancing was an important accomplishment, as we see in Pietro Longhi's The Dancing Lesson.*

## Everyday Life

The decadent spirit of 18th century Venice was manifest in its many cafés, theaters, parties, *ridotti*, and beautifully dressed aristocrats. However, among foreign visitors, Venice had a reputation for being not just beautiful, but also dirty and smelly. Arrangements for disposing of refuse were very basic. One English visitor described the Rialto area as "so dirtily kept … that disgust gets the better of every other sensation."

*A busy scene in a barber's shop in 18th century Venice.*

## Rococo Style

The main artistic style in Europe in the 18th century was the graceful, elegant style known as Rococo, to which Venetian artists such as Giambattista Tiepolo (1696–1770) and Rosalba Carriera (1675–1757) often added a touch of lavish theatricality or showmanship. Toward the end of the century, however, the Rococo gave way to the more restrained Neo-classical style, exemplified by the sculptor Antonio Canova (1757–1822).

*Art and crafts, like this lacquered cabinet, from the 18th century can now be seen in Venice's Museum of the Eighteenth Century, housed in the Ca' Rezzonico.*

## Music and Opera

Venetians were particularly fond of music, and especially opera, with both sopranos and *castrati* (castrated men) attracting devoted followers. The dominant musical figure of the time was composer Antonio Vivaldi (1678–1741). He became well known for operas and sacred music, and for instrumental works such as *The Four Seasons*.

*Antonio Vivaldi was nicknamed "The Red Priest," perhaps for the color of his hair.*

*Jacopo Tatti, better-known as Sansovino, worked on the square for over 30 years.*

### Architectural Developments

The first square, laid out in the 10th century, was about half the size of today's. The square's present appearance dates to the 16th century, when the Republic decided it needed a grand space that would reflect Venice's power and wealth. The architect given the task was Jacopo Sansovino (1486–1570). He designed the layout of the modern square — which in fact is far from square — and built the beautiful arcades on the north side. After his death, the work was taken over by Vincenzo Scamozzi, who

built the arcades on the south side of the square. In the early 19th century, a wing was built at the west end.

*At the top of the column of St. Mark stands a bronze winged lion, the emblem of Venice.*

**828** The relics of St. Mark are smuggled to Venice.

**1094** St. Mark's Basilica is completed.

**1529** Sansovino begins work on the square.

**1609** Galileo demonstrates his telescope

from the top of the bell tower.

**1638** Europe's first coffee house opens in the square.

**1720** Caffè Florian opens.

**1902** The campanile collapses.

**1912** The campanile reopens.

### Main Entrance to Venice

Until the 19th century, nearly all visitors to Venice arrived by sea, disembarking at the Molo San Marco. Between the Molo and the square lies the smaller

**1922** The Museo Correr, a museum dedicated to the city's history, opens in the square.

**1989** A Pink Floyd concert fills the area around St. Mark's Square with over 200,000 people.

**2002** Terrible flooding in the area.

piazzetta, with its two tall granite columns of St. Mark and St. Theodore. This was where executions took place in medieval times, and it is said that superstitious Venetians still avoid walking between the columns.

# St. Mark's

*St. Mark's Square has been a source of inspiration to painters for centuries.*

*Every summer, hundreds of thousands of tourists flock to the square — and nearly as many pigeons!*

I n a city full of narrow alleyways and out-of-the-way little squares, the grandeur and expanse of St. Mark's Square are unique. The focus of the square is undoubtedly St. Mark's Basilica, one of the most remarkable Christian monuments in the world. Its architecture and decoration provide vivid evidence of Venice's long association with the East. With the Basilica standing imperiously at the east end and the magnificent campanile soaring over it, the square has been at the center of Venetian life for over a thousand years, being the principal venue for festivals, games, and political events. Napoleon called it "the finest drawing room in Europe," and the square is still one of Venice's main attractions.

*In the 18th century, Francesco Guardi painted many views of the square.*

## St. Mark's Basilica

The basilica that dominates the square is the third church to be built on the site. The first basilica was built in the 9th century, to house the remains of St. Mark, but burnt down. Its replacement was demolished in the 11th century to make way for the magnificent building that visitors admire today. Its five domes, and the Greek-cross shape of its floor plan, show the influence of Byzantine and Oriental architecture.

*Beautiful mosaics, like this one of Archangel Michael, cover the domes, walls, and floor of the Basilica.*

This magnificent building provided the perfect setting for many of the official ceremonies of the Republic, and still today is a splendid backdrop to the square.

*Perhaps the most beautiful item inside the Basilica is the Pala d'Oro, a gold altarpiece made in the 10th century.*

*The horses of St. Mark's have long been a symbol of the city's independence. Seized by the French in 1797, they were returned to the city in 1815, an occasion which Vincenzo Chilone depicts in detail in this painting.*

*Famous visitors to Florian's over the years include Lord Byron, Charles Dickens, Richard Wagner, and more recently, Mikhail Gorbachov and Brad Pitt.*

## Café Society

Venice's first coffee house opened in the 17th century. A century later, there were no fewer than 24 such places in the square. During the 18th century, coffee houses became popular places to play cards, talk, and even meet secret lovers. Venice's most celebrated coffee house is Florian's, in the south arcade. Opposite is its rival, the Caffè Quadri.

*Open-air music adds to the atmosphere of Venice's café society.*

# Square

## The Clocktower

The ornate, Renaissance clocktower on the north side of the square was built at the end of the 15th century by Mauro Coducci. At the top of the tower are two large bronze figures known as the *Mori*, or "Moors," which strike the bell on the hour.

*The clock face displays not only the time of day but also the signs of the zodiac.*

## Floods

The square is generally one of the first places to suffer at *acqua alta*, or high tide. In recent years, the problem has become increasingly serious, with particularly bad floods in 2000 and 2002. Flooding has always been a threat to Venice's priceless art and architecture, and the fear is that with rising seas caused by global warming, the danger will only increase.

*When the square is under water, duckboards have to be laid out.*

## The Campanile

At 315 feet (96 m), the campanile (bell tower) towers over the square and provides magnificent views over the rooftops of the city and out into the lagoon. The original tower was built in the 8th century, as a lighthouse for ships in the lagoon, and was modified several times over the centuries. The present tower was opened on St. Mark's Day in 1912, having been rebuilt "dov'era e com'era" ("where it was and how it was") after its collapse 10 years earlier.

*On July 14, 1902, the campanile collapsed. It has since been rebuilt, and a lift added.*

BASILICA DI S.MARCO - VENEZIA
in occasione della
**visita al Campanile**
INTERO SERALE
ha versato l'offerta di **Euro 5,00**
BIGLIETTI DI CONTROLLO (DA CONSERVARE)
N° 28512  A    Offerta per il culto e per il decoro della Basilica GRAZIE

## THE RIALTO

**9th century** The Rialto area consists of a few small islands.

**1097** The first markets appear in the Rialto area.

**11th–12th centuries** The church of San Giacomo di Rialto is founded.

**1157** The first bank appears in the area.

**1228** The first German traders lease a building in the area.

**1264** The first permanent wooden bridge is built across the Grand Canal in the Rialto area.

**1310** A fire destroys the bridge.

**1444** A second wooden bridge collapses under the weight of a crowd watching the wedding of the Marchioness of Ferrara.

**1458** The wooden bridge is rebuilt.

**1514** A fire destroys most of the Rialto area.

**1588–91** A new stone bridge is built, to a design by Antonio da Ponte.

**1850** French poet Théophile Gautier visits the Rialto.

**21st century** The Rialto Bridge is a popular tourist attraction.

### The Competition

In the early 16th century, after a fire had destroyed most of the Rialto area, except the church of San Giacomo, it was agreed that a new stone bridge needed to be built across the Grand Canal. Many of the leading architects of the time submitted designs, including the celebrated Florentine sculptor and painter Michelangelo. Andrea Palladio, one of the best-known architects of the day, also produced a design, but this was rejected as being too complex. The architect finally chosen for the job was Antonio da Ponte (1512–97), who had already made a name for himself by rebuilding part of the Doge's Palace.

*Left: On one side of the bridge is carved this epitaph commemorating Doge Pasquale Cicogna, in whose period of office the stone bridge was built.*

*Below: Andrea Palladio's design proposed not so much a bridge as a magnificent commercial center spanning the Grand Canal.*

### Rialto Markets

The Rialto area has always been known as a shopping center, and is today particularly famous for its markets, especially the *Erberia* (fruit and vegetable market), and the *Pescheria* (fish market). Both are on the south side of the Grand Canal, and both are open to the public,

# The Rialto

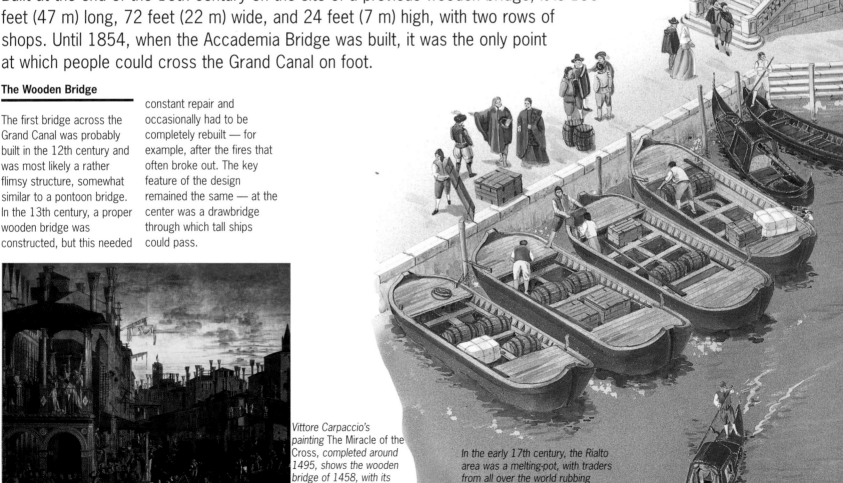

The Rialto had some of the best land for building and was probably one of the first areas to be inhabited. The name comes from the Italian words *rivo alto*, meaning "high bank." The area was Venice's first harbor — consignments of exotic spices, oils, and silks were unloaded from trading ships here and stored in warehouses known as *fondachi*. The Rialto became Venice's busiest center for every sort of commercial enterprise, including banks and insurance companies. The focus of the area now is the magnificent Rialto Bridge across the Grand Canal. Built at the end of the 16th century on the site of a previous wooden bridge, it is 156 feet (47 m) long, 72 feet (22 m) wide, and 24 feet (7 m) high, with two rows of shops. Until 1854, when the Accademia Bridge was built, it was the only point at which people could cross the Grand Canal on foot.

### The Wooden Bridge

The first bridge across the Grand Canal was probably built in the 12th century and was most likely a rather flimsy structure, somewhat similar to a pontoon bridge. In the 13th century, a proper wooden bridge was constructed, but this needed constant repair and occasionally had to be completely rebuilt — for example, after the fires that often broke out. The key feature of the design remained the same — at the center was a drawbridge through which tall ships could pass.

*Vittore Carpaccio's painting The Miracle of the Cross, completed around 1495, shows the wooden bridge of 1458, with its drawbridge to allow tall ships to pass through.*

*In the early 17th century, the Rialto area was a melting-pot, with traders from all over the world rubbing shoulders with craft workers, shipowners, and financiers.*

but as they open at the crack of dawn, most of the stalls are closed by noon. Locally grown asparagus and artichokes remain seasonal favorites. The French poet Théophile Gautier was so impressed by the range of items on sale when he visited in the middle of the 19th century that he wrote, "it is impossible to regale one's eyes more agreeably."

*Left: Stevedores unloaded heavy consignments from boats and took them to the Rialto markets and warehouses.*

## Goldsmiths on the Rialto

The buying and selling of gold has long been associated with the Rialto. When Antonio da Ponte's stone bridge was constructed, goldsmiths (in Venetian dialect, *oresi*) and silversmiths were among the first to set up business on it. A stone's throw from the bridge is the *Ruga degli Oresi*, the "Goldsmiths' Street." Other street names in the Rialto area reflect old businesses — the *Frezzerie* ("Arrowsmiths") and the *Mercerie* ("Clothsellers").

*The emblem of the Venice goldsmiths' association.*

## Hive of Activity

For many centuries, the Rialto was the financial heart of the city. Here could be found the moneylenders, bankers, and insurance agents who generated the city's wealth, as well as merchants from every part of the known world. The Rialto area was undoubtedly the epitome of Venice's cosmopolitan reputation. Next to the Rialto Bridge, a huge building known as the *Fondaco dei Tedeschi*

("Warehouse of the Germans"), was the headquarters for German merchants based in the city.

*Today, the bridge and whole Rialto area still hum with life from dawn to dusk, as tourists and locals look for bargains.*

## The Gobbo of the Rialto

This curious statue of a figure supporting a set of steps just by the Rialto Bridge symbolizes how Venetian traders thought of themselves — shouldering the heavy burden of taxes!

### Abdication of the Doge

When Napoleon's troops swept through northern Italy in 1797, the Venetian army tried to resist. Napoleon responded by ordering the capture of the city, signaling the end of the Republic's independent existence. In a meeting with the Great Council, Doge Manin is reported to have taken off his cap of office, saying "I shall not be needing it again."

*A coin minted in 1789, showing the lion of St Mark alongside the name of the last doge, Lodovico Manin.*

**1789 – 1870**

**1789** Revolution breaks out in France. Lodovico Manin is elected doge of Venice.

**1797** Doge Manin abdicates. Napoleon concedes Venice to Austria, in exchange for territory in Lombardy, further west.

### Napoleon Bonaparte

Napoleon Bonaparte came to power in France in the wake of the French Revolution of 1789. He overthrew the revolutionary government and became effectively the country's dictator, crowning himself

**1805–15** Venice is under French rule.

**1815** Venice is handed over to Austria at the Congress of Vienna.

**1822** Giuseppe Dal Niel buys the Palazzo Dandolo and converts it into a hotel, which later becomes the *Danieli*, Venice's most

luxurious place to stay.

**1844** Verdi's opera *Hernani* premieres at La Fenice.

**1846** Railroad link joins Venice to the mainland.

**1848** Uprising against Austrian rule.

Emperor in 1804. Napoleon modernized French law and education, but became embroiled in a series of wars with other European countries. He was finally defeated at the Battle of Waterloo in 1815, and forced into exile on the island of St. Helena.

**1858** The Fondaco dei Turchi, the old Turkish warehouse, is restored by the Austrians.

**1866** Venice joins the Kingdom of Italy.

**1870** After the unification, tourists visit Venice in increasing numbers.

*Napoleon Bonaparte (1769–1821).*

# The End of the Republic

**A**t the end of the 18th century, Venice tried to remain neutral as revolution in France was followed by a succession of European wars. However, since the Republic was no longer a military force to be reckoned with, it was powerless to prevent, first, invasion by the French, under Napoleon, and then occupation by the Austrians. Nor, as the 19th century progressed, could Venice remain untouched by developments, such as the Industrial Revolution, that were reshaping the rest of Europe. Indeed, the arrival of the railroad symbolized the end of centuries of Venetian independence. The fall of the Republic was a startling blow to the city, as it passed between Austria and France, and began a period of decline. When Venice emerged from Austrian rule in 1866, it became part of an Italy that had been a unified nation since 1861, and finally saw the end of its existence as an independent state.

### Napoleon in Venice

On May 12, 1797, Napoleon's troops invaded Venice, but by October of that year the city had been given to the Austrians as part of a peace deal. On leaving the city, French troops seized many of Venice's artistic treasures, such as the four bronze horses of St. Mark's.

French rule was reinstated from 1805 to 1815, and much of the booty returned. During this period, the Public Gardens were laid out, and many of the city's monasteries and churches were closed down. A new block was also added at the west end of St. Mark's Square — the Napoleon Wing.

*Napoleon arriving in Venice in November 1807 by Giuseppe Borsato. He stayed in the city for only ten days, but was enthusiastically received.*

## Under Austrian Rule

After the defeat of Napoleon at Waterloo, Venice passed into the hands of the Austrian Empire. The Austrians were never popular in Venice — one commentator of the time noted that, while the Venetians were "spontaneous," the Austrians were "dull and slow-witted." Although the Venetians resented the bureaucracy of Austrian rule, it did bring some practical benefits, such as the building in 1846 of the railroad bridge — the Ponte della Libertà ("Liberty Bridge") — linking Venice with mainland Italy.

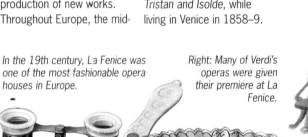

*Above: This iron bridge was built across the Grand Canal by Alfred Henry Neville, near the Accademia, in 1854. It has since been replaced by a more elegant wooden bridge.*

## Music

Opera was one of the most popular forms of entertainment in 19th-century Europe, with La Fenice one of the most important venues for the production of new works. Throughout Europe, the mid-19th century was the heyday of the Romantic movement, associated with composers such as the Italian Giuseppe Verdi (1813–1901) and the German, Richard Wagner (1813–83), who wrote part of his most famous opera, *Tristan and Isolde*, while living in Venice in 1858–9.

*In the 19th century, La Fenice was one of the most fashionable opera houses in Europe.*

*Right: Many of Verdi's operas were given their premiere at La Fenice.*

*Luchino Visconti's 1954 film Senso is about a love affair between a Venetian noblewoman and an Austrian army officer during the period of Austrian rule. This scene is set in the opera house.*

## The Romantic Writers

The early 19th century saw an influx of Romantic writers and poets into the city, including Byron, Shelley, and Musset, who recorded their views of Venice. Lord Byron (1788–1824) lived in Venice from 1816 until 1820, composing the fourth canto of his work, *Childe Harold's Pilgrimage*. In it he gave a vivid description of contemporary Venice, as it experienced the final stages of its decline:

*The spouseless Adriatic mourns her lord;*
*And annual marriage now no more renew'd,*

*Below: Venetian civilians battle against Austrian troops in St. Mark's Square in 1848.*

The Bucentaur lies rotting unrestor'd,
*Neglected garment of her widowhood!*

The English poet, Percy Bysshe Shelley (1792–1822) joined Byron in Venice, calling the city "the paradise of exiles," while Alfred de Musset (1810–57), the French poet and playwright, spent time at the famous Hotel Danieli, writing a number of articles about his experiences in the city.

## The Venetian Uprising

In March 1848, a rebellion against Austrian rule broke out in Venice, led by Daniele Manin (1804–57) and Nicolò Tommaseo (1802–74). On May 22 of

*Lord Byron wrote about the beauty of the Lido, well before it became a fashionable resort.*

that year they declared an independent Venetian Republic but, suffering from hunger and disease, the Venetian rebels were forced to surrender to Austrian troops in August 1849.

**THE LION OF ST. MARK.**

*Above: A cartoon from 1866, showing the Emperor of Austria, nearest the lion, handing over Venice to Napoleon III, who acted as mediator in the process of unification with Italy.*

*Right: A Venetian water-carrier, around 1850.*

## Life in the City

The 19th century was a period of modernization throughout Europe. In Venice, the Austrians brought improvements to the city's sanitation and water supply, but jobs were in short supply, as Trieste, along the coast, became the main port of the Austrian Empire.

## The Italian Risorgimento

At the beginning of the 19th century, the land that we now think of as Italy was divided into a number of separate states and kingdoms. The idea of a unified Italy was first proclaimed by Giuseppe Mazzini (1805–72), but the hero of the unification movement (known as the *Risorgimento*) was Giuseppe Garibaldi (1807–82), who formed an alliance with the Prussians to expel Austrian troops from the north. Italy was united in 1861, and when Venice became part of Italy in 1866, it entered into a spirit of rejuvenation and celebration. Victor Emmanuel II (1820–78), visiting the city in November 1866, was given a water-borne Venetian welcome, and by 1887 his statue, sculpted by Ettore Ferrari, stood on the Riva degli Schiavoni.

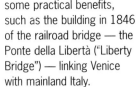

*Judith II by Gustav Klimt (1862–1918). His paintings were the talk of the 1910 Biennale.*

## 1870 – 1960

*A poster in the Art Deco style, advertising the 1928 exhibition.*

*Visitors to the first Biennale were encouraged by cheap rail fares and free entry to the exhibition itself.*

**1881** Venice is the second largest port in Italy.

**1895** The first Venice Biennale art exhibition is held.

**1907** Hotel Excelsior opens on the Lido.

**1908–10** Claude Monet paints a series of views of the city.

**1917** Work starts on the development of Marghera as a modern industrial port.

**1919** The Orient Express makes Venice a regular stop.

**1932** A road bridge is built between Venice and the mainland. The first Venice Film Festival is held.

**1934** Adolf Hitler meets Benito Mussolini in Venice.

**1936** The Palazzo della Cinema is built to house the Film Festival.

**1951** The Peggy Guggenheim Museum opens.

**1955** Katherine Hepburn and Rossano Brazzi film *Summertime* in Venice.

**1960** Marco Polo Airport opens, making Venice more easily accessible to foreign visitors.

## The Biennale

For the contemporary art world, Venice is especially significant as the venue for the Biennale — a major review of contemporary work from all over the world, held every two years. Over 200,000 visitors attended the first Biennale, which was opened by King Umberto I. Although it was originally seen as rather conservative, as the 20th century progressed the Biennale built up a reputation for showing the most innovative work of the times.

## Venice Film Festival

On August 6, 1932, the first Venice Film Festival opened, with the declared aim of raising "the new art of the cinema to the level of the other arts." Originally linked to the Biennale, *La Mostra*, as the festival is known to Venetians, was founded during the Fascist period. It is now an important international event.

*A poster advertising the very first Venice Film Festival.*

*In the film Summertime, Katherine Hepburn falls in love with a Venetian antique dealer.*

# Venice

## Harry's Bar

Undoubtedly the place to be seen sipping a Bellini cocktail is Harry's Bar, on the waterfront. Since it opened its doors in 1931, it has had many famous "regulars," including writer Ernest Hemingway, shipping magnate Aristotle Onassis, opera singer Maria Callas, and even British Prime Minister, Winston Churchill.

*Harry's Bar is famous for its carpaccio — wafer-thin slivers of steak, served with a special dressing and green salad — invented by its first owner, Giuseppe Cipriani, and named after the Venetian painter, Vittore Carpaccio.*

## Tourist Resort

Venice first became a tourist resort in the 18th century, when British aristocrats stopped off on their "Grand Tour" of the sights of Europe. In the 19th century, artistic figures such as Lord Byron, John Ruskin, and Richard Wagner visited the city, and as travel became easier, visitor numbers boomed. When the Suez Canal opened in 1869, Venice became a stopping-off point for travelers headed for the East in ocean liners. Another draw was the Orient Express, a luxury train that crossed Europe from Paris to Istanbul, stopping at Venice en route.

*In the 19th century, writers and artists helped put Venice on the tourist map.*

Venice's fortunes began to revive in the late 19th century, when the city became a magnet for leading literary and artistic figures, some of whom made their homes there. Its development was quick, and as the idea of establishing a tourist industry took hold, new luxury hotels sprang up in previously undeveloped areas, such as the Lido, and the city also became the venue for a range of prestigious artistic events. In the 20th century, the city emerged from two world wars virtually untouched, and areas such as Marghera and Mestre, on the mainland, became major industrial centers. The opening of an airport in 1960 confirmed that Venice, with all its history, was very much part of the modern world.

## Impressionist Venice

Venice has always been a favorite subject for painters. Toward the end of the 19th century, the soft light, subtle colors, and magnificent architecture of the city made Venice a perfect subject for

*Venice's warm colors, reflected in the water, fascinated Claude Monet, as seen in his painting of the Doge's Palace in 1908.*

French Impressionist painters such as Claude Monet (1840–1926) and Pierre Auguste Renoir (1841–1919).

The façade of the Basilica was covered up to protect it during World War I.

Right: Germany's Adolf Hitler visited Venice to seek an alliance with Italy's Fascist leader Benito Mussolini.

# in Fashion

## Venice during the Wars

The two world wars of the 20th century posed a major threat to Venice's artistic treasures. In 1915, the horses of St. Mark's were taken down and moved. During World War II, however, Venice was spared from bombing, apparently because it was on both the German and Allied lists of historic cities to be protected.

## Guggenheim Museum

Venice's association with modern art was strengthened by the foundation of the Peggy Guggenheim Museum. Peggy Guggenheim (1898–1979) was the niece of the wealthy industrialist Solomon Guggenheim. In 1949 she moved to Venice and bought the Palazzo Venier, on the Grand Canal, which houses her fine collection of work by modern masters.

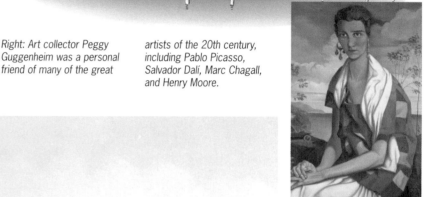

The Palazzo Venier is known as the Palazzo Leoni ("Palace of the Lions"), because its original owners kept pet lions chained up in the courtyard.

Right: Art collector Peggy Guggenheim was a personal friend of many of the great artists of the 20th century, including Pablo Picasso, Salvador Dalí, Marc Chagall, and Henry Moore.

## The Lido

The Venice Lido, an island 7 miles (11 km) long and 2 miles (3 km) wide in the lagoon, first became popular in the late 19th century, as the advent of sea-bathing turned it into one of Europe's most stylish resorts. Luxury hotels such as the Excelsior and the Grand Hotel des Bains attracted wealthy visitors from all over the world.

The Lido's attractions included fine beaches, casinos, and a golf course.

Left: The eyecatching façade of the Hotel Excelsior in the early 20th century.

### Torcello

Torcello is home to the oldest recorded building on the entire lagoon — the island's Byzantine cathedral of Santa Maria Assunta, built in 639. At one time, the most powerful and prosperous island on the lagoon, with a population of around 20,000, Torcello's decline can be dated to the time of Venice's rise to power, at the end of the Middle Ages. With a population of less than 100, the island now has an air of

*A mosaic of the Virgin and Child in the apse of Torcello Cathedral.*

## THE LAGOON

melancholy — but the serene church of Santa Fosca and the cathedral, with its beautiful mosaics and elaborately carved columns, are magnificent reminders of former glories.

**400s** Settlers begin to inhabit the lagoon.

**600s** The Sanctuary of Santa Maria is founded at Murano.

**1291** Glass furnaces are moved from Venice to Murano.

**1486** With the plague a

### The "Lace Island"

At the northern end of the lagoon is the island of Burano, clearly recognizable from a distance by its colorful houses and improbably angled church

recurrent hazard, the island of San Lazzaretto Nuovo is designated as Venice's quarantine station.

**1400s–1700s** Murano is Europe's leading center for glass production.

**16th century** Burano becomes Europe's leading center of lacemaking.

tower. By the 16th century, Burano had a reputation for producing the finest lace in Europe, including a particularly delicate form known as *punto in aria* ("points in the air"), but in the 18th century, foreign

**1577–92** The church of Il Redentore is built on the island of Guidecca.

**1807** The island of San Michele is chosen as the site for a new cemetery.

**1872** A school of lacemaking is founded on Burano, in an attempt to revive the art.

competition led to a slump in the market. Legend has it that Burano's houses were painted bright colors so that they could be recognized from a distance by fishermen returning home.

# The Lagoon

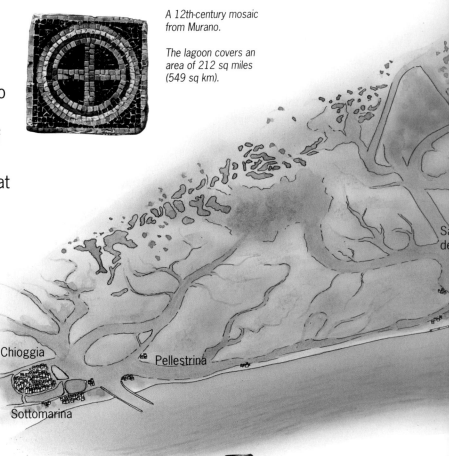

*A 12th-century mosaic from Murano.*

The lagoon covers an area of 212 sq miles (549 sq km).

The Venetian lagoon is virtually closed off from the Adriatic Sea by three long sand bars — the Lido di Venezia, the Lido di Jesolo, and Pellestrina. In the early Christian era, the islands of the lagoon were uninhabited, but in the 5th and 6th centuries groups of settlers came to the islands in search of security. For centuries, many of the 34 islands of the lagoon were thriving communities in their own right, and while two — Murano and Burano — are still known as craft centers, others such as Sant' Angelo della Polvere and Sant' Erasmo were equally prosperous in their day. Sadly, many of the islands of the lagoon are abandoned. At the southern tip of the lagoon, the town of Chioggia, once Venice's rival, survives as a fishing port, with its own version of the Lido at the resort of Sottomarina.

*Map labels:* Chioggia · Pellestrina · Sottomarina

*Left: Inside a glass workshop on Murano.*

### Murano

Murano, the largest of the islands in the lagoon, has been a center for the manufacture of glass since the late 13th century, when Venice's furnaces were

moved here to avoid the risk of fire. From the 15th to 18th centuries Murano was at the height of its powers, with a population of over 30,000, and had its own version of the *Libro d'Oro* ("Golden Book"), Venice's

register of noble families. Unlike the rest of Europe, here a young man did not need to belong to a glassmaking family to become an apprentice — enthusiasm and talent could make him a master

glassmaker. However, the Republic guarded such expertise so carefully that glassmakers were forbidden to emigrate.

*A brightly colored enameled glass flask, made around 1740.*

### The Living Lagoon

The lagoon is sustained by a delicate ecological balance. While the shallower areas (known as the "dead lagoon") are submerged only at high tide, the deeper waters (the "living lagoon") are home to a wide range of wildlife, from kingfishers and cormorants to shrimps and crabs. This is

**1971** The Venice in Peril charity is established, with the aim of preventing the threats posed by climate change and rising sea levels.

**1995** The Italian State auctions some minor treasures of the smaller islands.

*Delicate Burano lace.*

*Above: Vividly painted houses along the seafront at Burano.*

## "Island of the Dead"

The island of San Michele, northeast of Venice, became the city's main cemetery in the early 19th century. Alongside the citizens of Venice, many eminent modern authors and artists also chose to be buried here, including the poet Ezra Pound and the composer Igor Stravinsky.

*The grave of the Russian composer Igor Stravinsky (1882–1971).*

*Lacemakers used chairs with foot rests as they worked.*

## The Fishing Trade

The waters of the lagoon have always been rich fishing grounds. By the 16th century there was a powerful Fishermen's Guild, which advised the Senate on matters relating to the lagoon. At the southern tip of the lagoon is the small town of Chioggia, once a center for salt production, but since medieval times the home of a thriving fishing community.

*Left: A wealthy Venetian of the 18th century, out hunting duck on the lagoon, a popular sport of the time.*

*A fisherman with his catch of sardines.*

now threatened by pollution from industrial towns such as Marghera, while water traffic is eroding the sandbanks that provide a natural habitat for many species.

*The marshes of the lagoon provide rich pickings for herons.*

*Right: The façade of Palladio's Il Redentore is a superb example of Classical architecture.*

## Giudecca

The origin of the island's name has long been disputed. One school of thought argues that Giudecca refers to the Jewish community who lived here in medieval times. More likely, however, is the explanation that in the 9th century a group of aristocrats were banished here after being tried in court (*giudicato*). The island's most impressive monument is the church of Il Redentore, designed by Andrea Palladio and built in thanksgiving for the end of a plague that ravaged Venice in 1576.

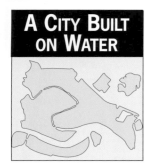

## A CITY BUILT ON WATER

**1100s** First historical reference to the gondola.

**1300** The city's first official regatta is held.

**1420** Building work begins on the Ca d'Oro.

**1493** The first women's regatta is held.

**1600s** An estimated 10,000 gondolas are in use on Venice's canals.

**1633** To curb the fashion for lavish decoration, the doge orders that all gondolas must be painted black.

**1825** The regatta becomes an annual event.

**Around 1900** The first steam-driven *vaporetti* appear on the Grand Canal.

**1988** The Italian government launches a campaign to clean up pollution in the lagoon.

**1990s** Studies show that vibrations from the city's water buses are causing damage to the foundations of buildings along the Grand Canal.

The Women's Regatta by Gabriele Bella. Every year a woman's race is held in honor of Béatrice d'Este, wife of the 15th-century Duke of Milan.

### Regattas

In a city where sporting possibilities are limited, Venice's many annual regattas are one of the main attractions. The first boat races probably date back to medieval times, when they served as a form of military exercise. Events are now held between March and September each year. One of these, *La Sensa*, takes place on Ascension Day, and commemorates the ancient ceremony of the doge's "marriage with the sea" (see pages 22–23). Meanwhile the *Vogalonga*, first organized in 1974 to promote Venetian-style rowing, is an 18-mile (29 km) round trip from St. Mark's Basin to the island of Burano. The largest event, however, is the *Regatta Storica* ("Historical Regatta"), which takes place on the first Sunday in September.

# A City Built on Water

*Below: A poster advertising the Historical Regatta.*

**F**or Venetians, the water has always been their lifeblood. The canals of Venice, of which there are over a hundred, date back to the 5th century when the early settlers first began building in the swampy marshes of the lagoon. Scores of separate islands were linked together with bridges and canals, and divided in two by the Grand Canal, which snakes through the heart of the city forming a backward "S." Over the centuries some of the city's most stunning buildings were constructed along the Grand Canal, while the smaller canals, many only 13–16 feet (4–5 m) wide, formed a dense urban network within the city. The Venetians have over a thousand years' experience of living on the water, and in that time they have developed many traditions that reflect their unique lifestyle. These range from their own methods of transportation, such as the world-famous gondola and the public water buses, to spectacular ceremonies to celebrate the city's relationship with the sea.

## Gondolas and Gondoliers

The long, slender shape of the gondola makes it perfectly suited to navigating the city's intricate network of narrow canals. The boats, produced in yards known as *squeri*, are about 35 feet (10 m) long. The six metal strips on the bow are said to represent the six districts (or *sestrieri*) into which the city is divided. In the 15th and 16th centuries, every wealthy family had its own private gondola and gondolier, or oarsman. Today, gondolas are used mainly by tourists, and the number of gondoliers, many of whom still dress in the traditional black pants, hooped vest, and straw hat, has shrunk to just a few hundred.

*Above: One of the last gondola yards in Venice. The gondolas are worked on by the canalside in summer, and in the wooden shed in the winter.*

*Left: In the 16th century in winter months, some gondolas were equipped with a felze, a small cabin that enabled passengers to keep warm and dry.*

*For centuries, the profession of gondolier has been passed down from father to son. Only native Venetians can apply for a license.*

*Before the main events in September's Historical Regatta, Venetians row down the Grand Canal in fancy dress. Luca Carlevaris captured this scene in his painting entitled* A Regatta on the Grand Canal (1711).

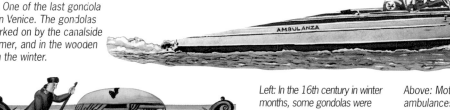

*Vaporetto route 1 travels the length of the Grand Canal.*

### The Grand Canal

The Grand Canal, referred to by locals as the *Canalazzo*, meanders for about 2.5 miles (4 km) through the center of Venice. It used to be the main waterway for merchant vessels bound for the Rialto and, even today, it remains the city's main artery. One visitor, as long ago as 1495, described it as "the most beautiful street in the world," and it still provides ravishing views of many of Venice's most splendid palaces.

## Traveling around the City

Gondolas provide a romantic, if expensive, means of traveling around Venice. Most Venetians, however, prefer to take a *vaporetto*, the diesel-powered water buses that serve the Grand Canal, the lagoon, and its islands. There is also the double-decker *motonavi*, or the *traghetto*, a kind of ferry (standing room only) that crosses the canal at seven points. Water taxis and motor boats also plow the Venetian canals.

*Above: Motorized water ambulances provide the quickest route to Venice's main hospital, in the Campo Santi Giovanni e Paolo.*

*Above: At the bow of the traditional funeral barge was a gold-winged angel. Following the funeral barge would be a cortège of gondolas with mourners.*

### The Big Freeze

In 1708 the lagoon froze over, enabling Venetians to walk to the mainland. In particularly harsh winters, it is not unknown for the Grand Canal to freeze over too, making it impassable by boat. The traditional solution were pairs of elementary skates, probably copied from the ones Venetian merchants had seen in northern Europe.

### Funeral Barges

In death, as in life, tradition has always linked Venetians to the water. Although most Venetians are now buried on the mainland, in the past, bodies were taken across the water to the island of San Michele (see page 37) on richly decorated funeral barges.

*An intrepid 18th-century Venetian ventures out on the ice.*

*The Ca' d'Oro (the "Golden House") is a fine example of the 15th century architectural style known as Venetian Gothic. It was built for Marino Contarini, who wanted it to be the most beautiful palace on the Grand Canal.*

Below: The wavy roofline is a distinctive feature of the Gothic church of the Frari.

## Byzantine Influence

In the early years of its history, Venice was closely linked to the Byzantine Empire, with its center at Constantinople (now Istanbul). Masons and mosaicists came from Constantinople and Greece, or from Ravenna, further down the Italian coast, to work in the first churches, both in Venice and on islands such as Torcello in the lagoon. The church of San Giacomo di Rialto is a typical Byzantine design — its floor plan is based on a Greek cross rather than the more elongated Latin cross. The supreme example of Byzantine architecture, however, is St. Mark's Basilica, with its five domes and beautiful mosaics.

Above: The design of St. Mark's Basilica is influenced by the Church of the Apostles in Constantinople.

## VENETIAN ARCHITECTURE

Delicately carved tracery from the 15th century Gothic Palazzo Cavalli Franchetti.

**600s** The Byzantine church of San Nicolò dei Mendicoli is founded.

**1260** Santa Maria della Carità is founded, the first of Venice's *scuole grandi*.

**1481–9** The church of Santa Maria dei Miracoli is built.

**1500s** Sansovino designs

the new Zecca (mint) building in St. Mark's Square.

**1631** The Basilica of Santa Maria della Salute is built in thanksgiving for the end of the plague.

**1750** Completion of the Ca' Rezzonico.

**1966** Carlo Scarpa

## Gothic Style

The Gothic style, which in much of western Europe is associated mainly with churches, can be seen in Venice in some of the city's magnificent private houses and palaces. One fine example is the Ca' d'Oro on

the Grand Canal, but probably the most obviously Gothic building is the Doge's Palace (see pages 10–11) itself, with its elegant latticework and minutely finished details. Many of Venice's churches are also in Gothic style, such as the brick church of

# Venetian

**V**enice's architecture is without doubt one of its most remarkable cultural treasures, as well as a reflection of the city's history. Much of the early city was built on timber piles which were forced into the bottom of the lagoon, proving a resilient basis for years of successive building work. The Byzantine influences visible in the oldest buildings are evidence of links with the eastern Mediterranean in the early medieval period, while the opulent palaces and magnificent churches built in Gothic and Renaissance styles from the 14th through the 17th centuries, reflect the time of the city's greatest wealth and power. Venice's island situation means that space for new development has always been at a premium, and at the beginning of the 21st century there is a delicate balance between the need to redevelop some areas of the city, while preserving its unique architectural legacy.

## Baroque Period

During the 17th century, the time of the Baroque style, relatively few major building projects were undertaken. However, Venice does have one Baroque masterpiece — the Basilica of Santa Maria della Salute, built by

Baldassare Longhena (1598–1682), across the Grand Canal from St. Mark's Square. The church has all the grandeur and formal complexity that are the hallmarks of the style, and its interior is a superb example of dramatic lighting.

A view of Santa Maria della Salute, painted around 1737 by Michele Marieschi.

creates a new entrance to the Institute of Architecture.

**1996** Santiago Calatrava proposes a design for a fourth bridge over the Grand Canal.

**2000** Spanish architect Enrico Miralles Moya wins approval for a radical plan to redevelop an area on each side of the Giudecca canal.

Santa Maria Gloriosa dei Frari (usually known simply as "the Frari"), built on a Latin cross plan, with a tall nave and vaulted roof.

*Right: A detail from Titian's The Assumption, painted between 1516 and 1518. It is one of the masterpieces in the Frari.*

*Begun in 1565, the façade of San Giorgio Maggiore shows the influence of classical temples, such as the Pantheon in Rome.*

# Architecture

## 19th Century Contributions

The 19th century in Venice was a time of renovation and refinement rather than major new building projects. Some of the arcades lining St. Mark's Square were adapted for use as shops or cafés, and the city was embellished with elegant "street furniture," in wrought or cast iron. Two new bridges, the Scalzi and Accademia, were built over the Grand Canal in this period.

*One of the 19th-century street lamps in the piazzetta, in front of the Doge's Palace.*

## Modern Architecture

The centuries have taken their toll on Venice, and it is no easy matter to restore the city. Le Corbusier (1887–1965), the Swiss architect and town planner, made plans for a new hospital in the Cannaregio area, but he died before the project could be built. Another missed opportunity was that of Frank Lloyd Wright's (1867–1959) plans for student housing in the city in 1953. However, Spanish architect Enrico Miralles Moya (1955–2000)

## The Venetian Palace

The basic plan of Venice's palaces changed little over the centuries. The typical palace had entrances for those arriving by land or water. On the ground floor was a large hallway, from which a grand staircase led up to the *piano nobile* (the elegant first floor), where there was a salon, with a gallery overlooking the canal and suites of smaller private rooms off it. Servants' quarters were in the attic, and above this was the *altana*, a terraced roof where noblewomen could relax in the sun and "take some air."

*Right: Statue of the Virgin and Child from the church of Santa Maria dei Miracoli.*

*The Ca' Rezzonico on the Grand Canal was the scene of many majestic balls and receptions during the Venetian Republic.*

produced plans to redevelop one of Venice's run-down areas, using materials such as concrete and steel. Work is now underway to create a new urban waterfront with shops, libraries, banks, bars, and restaurants.

## The *Scuole*

Dating back as far as the 13th century, the *scuole* were fraternities that supported good causes, organized official celebrations, and could even lobby the Senate. There were six *scuole grandi*, whose members included

## Renaissance and Palladian Style

The 15th century saw the arrival of the Renaissance style, for example at the church of Santa Maria dei Miracoli in Cannaregio, which has classical pilasters and marble cladding. The first great architect of Renaissance Venice was Jacopo Sansovino, who designed St. Mark's Square (see pages 28–29), and the magnificent library bearing his name, the Libreria

Sansoviniana, opposite the Doge's Palace. The most celebrated architect of the period, though, was Andrea Palladio, who built two great Venetian churches: Il Redentore on Giudecca (see page 37) and San Giorgio Maggiore (above), across the water from the Doge's Palace, and notable for its un-Venetian restraint and simplicity.

*Andrea Palladio (1508–80) was a keen student of the architecture of classical Rome.*

the great and good of the city, and many more humble *scuole minori*, whose members might all be from the same trade guild, or have some other connection. The wealth of

*A view of the Scuola della Misericordia.*

the *scuole grandi* allowed them to commission magnificent buildings as their headquarters, but all the *scuole* were closed down in 1806.

*Above left: The "Theater of the World," a floating exhibition hall, was designed by Italian architect Aldo Rossi in 1979.*

*Above: The picturesque wooden Accademia Bridge was built in 1932 to replace a 19th-century iron version, built under Austrian rule.*

**1960 –
PRESENT**

**1966** The worst floods in Venice's history.

**1970** Filmmaker Luchino Visconti makes his version of *Death in Venice*.

**1978** Cardinal Luciani, archbishop of Venice, is elected pope and takes the name John Paul I. He dies after only 33 days in office.

**1979** The Venice Carnival is revived.

**1988** The prototype of the MOSE flood barrier is launched.

**1989** 150,000 tourists visit Venice on a single day — the highest recorded figure.

**1992** Proposals are put forward for a metro system under the lagoon.

**1995** Centenary of the first Venice Biennale art exhibition.

**1996** Fire destroys La Fenice opera house.

**2003** Italian prime minister Silvio Berlusconi lays the foundation stone of the MOSE project, designed to save the lagoon from tidal flooding.

*For all its history, Venice is a major center for exhibitions of modern art.*

## Entertainment and Art

Venice offers tourists and residents every type of entertainment. La Fenice opera house is currently being rebuilt with plans to reopen in December 2003. Meanwhile its rival, the Malibran Theater, built in

*Above: Inside one of Venice's bustling osterie.*

1677, has recently opened its doors again to the theater-loving public. Live music can be heard at the Goldoni Theater, and occasionally in the churches and *scuole* around the city. In addition to hosting the Biennale, the city also has a plentiful supply of private art galleries, and there are regular exhibitions of modern art and design at the Ca' Pesaro, with its paintings by Matisse, Chagall, and Klimt, and at the Fortuny Museum.

Venetians are also fond of spending time in their local *osteria* — a bar where traditional snacks (*ciccheti*) can be nibbled, or local dishes such as salt cod (*baccalà*), and rice with peas (*risi e bisi*) enjoyed.

# Venice Today

With the arrival of the 21st century, Venice is a fragile city faced with increasing challenges and problems. Since few industries other than tourism provide long-term employment, the city's population is now in decline, as young people leave to look for jobs elsewhere. Those still living in the city have to live with the constant threat of flooding, while striving to preserve their priceless artistic and architectural legacy. New schemes to prevent flooding and for the regeneration of some of the less glamorous areas of the city seem to promise a brighter future, and guarantee its survival into the new millennium.

## Separatist Bid

In 1996, Umberto Bossi, the leader of Italy's Northern League (a political party), proclaimed Venice the capital of "Padania," his imaginary new republic, split off from the rest of Italy. In 1997, some of Bossi's supporters climbed to the top of the campanile in St. Mark's Square, unfurled a banner and announced, "The Most Serene Venetian Army has liberated St. Mark's Square." It seems, however, that they have little public support.

*Supporters of "Padania" flew the red and yellow banner of St. Mark from the top of the campanile.*

## Acqua Alta

When high tide, low air pressure, and high winds combine, as they do every 20 to 30 years, they can lead to floods of about 3 feet (0,9 m), and every two centuries or so they can cause flooding on the scale of November 1966. The next major flood is predicted for 2030, and plans are being drawn up to avoid a repetition of the catastrophe of 1966. The MOSE project, an acronym for *Modulo Sperimentale Elettro Meccanico*, involves placing 80 mobile flood barriers in the lagoon. However, some environmental groups fear that the project will disturb the lagoon's ecosystem.

*Left: Life in Venice was paralyzed in November 1966 when it was hit by the worst flooding in its history.*

## The Flood of 1966

Venice has always been vulnerable to the flooding that occasionally occurs between October and April. On November 4, 1966, however, the city was struck by the worst floods on record, with St. Mark's Square under 4 feet (1,2 m) of water. Nobody was killed, but more than 5,000 people were made homeless, many artworks were damaged, and there was extensive pollution as domestic fuel tanks were smashed. Electricity had to be cut off and telephone lines were out. It took more than a week for the waters to subside. After further floods the following winter, the Venetian authorities began looking at long-term measures to prevent a major catastrophe.

*Below: A diagram of part of the massive retractable flood barriers proposed for project MOSE.*

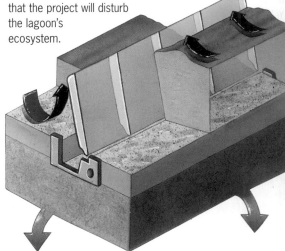

## Preserving Venice

Already in the 19th century, there was a growing awareness of the need to preserve many buildings in Venice. Following the floods of 1966, the international organization UNESCO launched a campaign to help the Italian government in safeguarding Venice, and for much of the time since then, the Americans and British have been at the forefront of conservation and restoration projects. The Venice in Peril Fund was founded by Sir Ashley Clarke, former British ambassador to Italy, with its first project being the restoration of the church of the Madonna dell' Orto in Cannaregio. Now, however, environmental problems are a leading issue, but the restoration work on many of Venice's monuments still goes on.

*Clothes hanging out to dry in Calle Michelangelo, on Giudecca.*

*Above: Colorful clothes mask unfinished restoration work on the 13th-century Scuola dei Varoteri.*

### Life Goes On

Only about 58,000 people actually live in Venice today (compared with twice that number in 1945). Many see this population depletion as evidence of Venice's death as a "living city." Although many non-tourist businesses have left for the mainland, alongside traditional crafts such as glassmaking, new ones have also developed — for example Venice is now a center for the production of marbled paper.

### Tourism

Over 12 million tourists visit Venice every year, and on a given day at the height of the season, there may be as many as 100,000 tourists in the city. At times it seems the place can barely cope. Yet in the 1990s it was even suggested that Venice should be the host for Expo 2000, with a projected 45 million people visiting the show over four months — a proposal that was firmly rejected. The annual influx of tourists provides work for restaurants, hotels, and souvenir stores — of which there are said to be over 400 — and it keeps the remaining glassblowers and lacemakers in business. About one-third of Venice's population works in tourism in some form, but not surprisingly, the authorities are trying to broaden the city's economy by encouraging new businesses, particularly hi-tech enterprises, to make Venice their base.

*Above: A scene from the James Bond film Moonraker, part of which was filmed in Venice.*

*Left: Johnny Depp arriving at the 60th Venice Film Festival in August 2003.*

### Film Star Venice

Venice has provided the setting for so many films that it can claim to be a star in its own right. Film adaptations of books set in the city include Luchino Visconti's version of Thomas Mann's *Death in Venice* (1970), set for the most part in the Grand Hotel des Bains on the Lido, and the 1997 film of Henry James's *The Wings of the Dove*. In the 1950s, Visconti's *Senso* (see page 33) was a poignant love story set in 19th-century Venice, while for more recent films such as *Moonraker* (1979) and *Indiana Jones and the Last Crusade* (1989), the city provided a stylish backdrop. Federico Fellini's *Casanova* (1976), meanwhile, charted the adventures of the 18th-century libertine, and Nic Roeg's *Don't Look Now* (1973) captured the city's menacing aspects by placing the action in a typical winter fog.

*Many tourists, known as "pendolari" to the Venetians, are on day trips to the city.*

*Left: At the height of the tourist season, stalls selling souvenirs can make Venice's narrow streets almost impassable.*

# Index